How to Become a Pharmacist:

The Ultimate Guide

Everything You want to know from Job Description to Training, Degree Requirements, Pharm D Certification, Schools, Salary, AND what to know about Pharmacy Techs and Technician Assistants – All Covered!

By Denise Jackson

Disclaimer and legal notice

- The information in this book is provided and sold with the knowledge that the publisher and author do not offer any legal, medical or other professional advice. In the case of a need for any such expertise consult with the appropriate professional. This book does not contain all information available on the subject. This book has not been created to be specific to any individual's or organizations' situation or needs.

- Although the author and publisher have made every effort to ensure that the information in this book was correct at press time, the author and publisher do not assume and hereby disclaim any liability to any party for any loss, damage, or disruption caused by errors or omissions, whether such errors or omissions result from negligence, accident, or any other cause.

- This book is not intended as a substitute for the medical advice of physicians. The reader should regularly consult a physician in matters relating to health and particularly with respect to any symptoms that may require diagnosis or medical attention.

Contents

Introduction

Chances are, if you're reading this, you have already given at least some thought to becoming a pharmacist. You're fascinated with chemistry, science, health care, and the many ways in which medicine relieves symptoms to curing diseases.

This book is designed to provide you with all of the information and understanding of the process that you will need to follow to become a highly sought after pharmacist. We'll cover a broad range of topics in the field in a sustained and clear fashion, explaining the basics of everything you need to know, from A to Z, on becoming a pharmacist--and the vast potential of career choices in the field. We'll provide a variety of examples of strategies and tips that can be applied in your real life situation to enhance your potential and education. Whether you know nothing about the pharmacy field or a little bit here and there, this book will serve as a valuable resource and tool that will guide you along your path to obtaining your certification and licensure.

The field of pharmacy is an amazing profession, and not only offers huge earning potential but you also get the opportunity to help people. If you like the idea of making creative and challenging decisions every day, helping others to solve their problems, and earning a lucrative living, then becoming a pharmacist may be right up your alley.

How to Become a Pharmacist: the Ultimate Guide, will show you exactly what you need to know to become a knowledgeable and respected pharmacist. You'll learn what the job entails, educational requirements, and what training or experience you'll need to attain the financial and career stability you're looking for. This book focuses not only on becoming a pharmacy technician, assistant, or pharmacist, but other lucrative careers in the field of pharmacy, including a brief visit to the world of pharmacology.

Have you ever wondered exactly what that guy wearing the white lab coat does behind that glass other than count pills? How much does he have to know to do his job reliably and effectively?

If becoming a pharmacist is your idea of a dream job, this book will prove an indispensable guide to help you navigate and prepare for one of the most exciting, challenging, and lucrative careers out there. The potential for the field is unlimited. There will *always* be a need for pharmacists, and your certification and license will stand you in good stead for a career that can span decades.

How to Become a Pharmacist: the Ultimate Guide will help you understand the world of a pharmacist and the responsibilities of the position. Learning where the best jobs are, and why, will enable you to make good choices when it comes to job opportunities and earning potential.

Each chapter in this book provides valuable information based on its topic. You don't have to read the chapters in order if you don't want to. However, the book is organized by topics to provide a logical flow of information that follows the traditional pathway for your journey from start to finish. We'll cover topics that include, but are not limited to, job responsibilities, where the best jobs are, who is responsible for what, earning potential, and education basics. We'll talk about suggestions for undergrad classes that can help pave your way, as well as self-tests that you can utilize in preparing for enrollment in a pharmacy college. Finally, we'll wrap with a variety of tips and strategies to help you prepare for (and pass!) your certification and licensure as a pharmacy technician, assistant, or doctor of pharmacy--and beyond.

The overall goal of this book is to help you visualize that your job as a pharmacist is the perfect choice for you, and then show you how to get there. So let's get started!

Chapter 1: Exploring the Field of Pharmacy

Introduction

So, you're interested in becoming a pharmacist? Okay, so the first thing you should know is the origination and meaning of the word pharmacy--meaning the art or practice or preparations of drugs, while pharmacology is defined as the study of drugs.

The prefix "pharma" originates from the ancient Greek term *pharmakon*, which literally meant either a remedy or a poison, although using today's modern usage, the word implies "drug." The term pharmacy originates from both Medieval Latin (*pharmacia*) and Greek (*pharmakeia*).

Did you know that the study of pharmacology or the composition and properties of herbal concoctions dates back to the Middle Ages? So does pharmacy--the practice of measuring, preparing, and delivering of these drugs or medicines to people. Back in the old days, a pharmacist may have been called a lot of not-very-nice-names such as sorcerer, enchanter, a poisoner, or even a witch! Can you imagine hanging your shingle over your new drugstore or pharmacy today and labeling it "Sorcerer" with an arrow pointing down to your door! Not so much.

The use of the word "pharmacy" as a location where drugs or medicines were prepared and offered to the public goes back centuries, though the *practice* dates back to the 15th century and beyond. The earliest usage of the term "pharmacist" was found in an English publication of a novel in 1834. What? A novel? Yes, you read that correctly. The novel was called *The Last Days of Pompeii*, written by Edward Bulwer Lytton, and in it is found one of the first references to what we know today as a modern pharmacist.

Actually, according to the Royal Pharmaceutical Society, professionals in the field practiced their craft thousands of years

BC, in an art form we now refer to as good old-fashioned folk medicine. Back then, these individuals specialized in the cultivation of herbs and ingredients to create treatments for their patients (some of which worked out okay; others not so much).

In fact, ancient papyrus scrolls dating back to the ancient Egyptians (circa 1500 BC) made mention of such "medicine preparers" given the name *Pastophor*. Such individuals were highly regarded and respected in their day.

Ancient Chinese also studied the properties of hundreds of herbs and around the same time (1500-2000 BC) had a book to rely on that contained the descriptions and medicinal properties of approximately 350 plant-based drugs (the first version of the *Pen T'sao*, originally penned by Shen Nung).

A note of interest: The old term "apothecary" is often misused as a reference to a pharmacist, but the apothecary was neither a pharmacist, a druggist, nor a chemist. The apothecary was a person who specialized in spices, though one who also occasionally traded in already-prepared medicines and crude forms of drugs. For a fascinating glimpse into history and the history of the field of pharmacy, check out the Royal Pharmaceutical Society and their page regarding the history of the field.[1]

In some ways, you can say that the fields of pharmacy and pharmacology are related like siblings, which is why in this section we'll talk a bit about both. In learning about the field, you'll soon understand why they're so often linked hand-in-hand, and indeed why many people often interchange the terms to mean the same thing. They don't.

Something to remember: At its most basic description, **pharmacology** is a science that studies, understands, and

---

[1] http://www.rpharms.com/about-pharmacy/history-of-pharmacy.asp

enhances the action of drugs and/or medications on biological systems. **Pharmacy** or pharmaceutics defines the science surrounding the preparation and dispensing of medicines and drugs.

In its earlier usage, the term "pharmacology" defined the scientific discipline that studies the effects of active chemicals on biological organisms, including us humans. Today, the field of pharmacology spans a wide range of studies and research including the biological effects of certain drugs and medications on people, their molecular makeup, functions, and mechanisms, as well as how natural and/or synthetic drugs can affect the human body.

If you like unraveling mysteries, there's nothing quite so fascinating than delving into the behavioral as well as physiological effects that certain chemical properties can have on the human body. As a pharmacist, this knowledge will stand you in good stead. The field of pharmacy combines several different science and medical disciplines that include cellular and molecular biology, knowledge of biochemistry, and of course, anatomy and physiology. With such knowledge, you have the capability of providing medical knowledge and support to hundreds, if not thousands, of patients throughout your career as a pharmacist.

As an interdisciplinary field, pharmacy and pharmacology offer exciting, challenging, and continually advancing career options as new technologies, discoveries, and research opportunities enhance our knowledge of drugs and medications.

Exploring the field of pharmacy is the first step you'll take on your journey to making choices that will welcome you as a valuable member of the scientific community--one who can be productive, rewarded, and recognized for your efforts. So let's get started on our journey toward understanding the world of a pharmacist.

5

Understanding the world of a pharmacist

For those who are extremely motivated, curious, and devoted to areas of science, chemistry, and medicine (and health and wellness), your opportunities and the challenges you will experience in the pharmaceutical world will definitely get your blood pumping. As a pharmacist or pharmacy technician, you have the potential to be part of a caregiving process and team of professionals that encourages and supports physical, mental, and emotional health and wellness for society.

Your knowledge as a pharmacist is not only limited to human medical conditions, but can also be used in fields of dentistry, nursing, and yes, for our four-legged and feathered friends in veterinary medicine. As a pharmacist, your studies will provide the knowledge on everything from the effect a specific chemical agent can have on sub-cellular mechanisms to the hazards in the widespread use of herbicides and pesticides, or in providing and developing prevention treatments through drug therapies to those diagnosed with disease processes.

First, let's delve a little deeper into two major fields that are closely related yet distinct in their processes. So, what's the difference between a pharmaceutical and pharmacology student.

Something to remember: Keep in mind that a pharmacist is a separate discipline found *within* the health sciences studies, which includes pharmacy or pharmaceuticals. Pharmacology fields are often considered a *discipline of pharmacy*. As such, pharmacology is vital in the study of pharmacy, but the two disciplines are, as emphasized earlier, distinct. You can practice patient-oriented pharmacy (or pharmaceuticals) as a pharmacist, as well as biomedical sciences and scientific methods that involve the field of pharmacology, and receive separate degrees unique to these fields.

However, in order to enhance your understanding of the vast career potential in the field, and because your options are plentiful, we want to briefly cover the field of pharmacology here. Why? Because pharmacists and pharmacy students *do* transition into the world of pharmacology, and it's good to know your options.

The field of pharmacology is continually expanding. The newest areas, providing nearly limitless potential in knowledge, scientific research, and capabilities, include genomic research as well as proteomic advancements and approaches to a number of therapeutic treatments. Huh? Let's put it this way:

As a student of pharmacology, your potential contributions to the field could very well be the next breakthrough in the treatment of, or therapeutic approaches to, disease processes or the prevention of an illness. You have the potential to help develop a cure for common conditions today including cancer, neurodegenerative conditions like Parkinson's disease, and even cognitive and degenerative conditions like Alzheimer's. Needless to say, the capacity, studies, and research in this field are exciting and offer huge potential to any student who desires to make a difference!

Think of yourself as an ultra-modern detective who has the potential of discovering and unraveling the mysteries of drug action processes. Discover new treatments or therapies, or participate in the development of new drugs or other medicinal products that ultimately improve quality of life or save lives. In recent years, the headway and progress made in the development of new drugs and how they act and interact with living biological systems is nearly endless, and enhance our fundamental understanding of life processes.

What's the potential in the field of pharmacology and why should I know it? After all, I want to be a pharmacist!

The potential in the fields of pharmacology or pharmacy are huge! Whether you want to become a Doctor of Pharmacy (Pharm.D.), a pharmacy technician, or you decide you want to go into pharmaceutical sales or management, your options are nearly endless. The pharmaceutical industry is a highly sought-after field that offers nearly limitless potential. The same applies if you want to advance your knowledge, education, and career and later also enter the field of pharmacology.

You may be interested to know that both these degrees (pharmacy and pharmacology) begin with a focus on a generalized understanding of science. When you start out as a pharmacy student, you'll learn about human physiology, microbiology, and biochemistry. The same subjects apply to pharmacology. The point is, you're exploring options, not only to become a pharmacist, but in determining how high and how far you can go in this lucrative industry.

As a pharmacology student, you can focus on a number of health fields including, but not limited to, **endocrine pharmacology**, defined as the study of interactions and actions of medications or drugs derived from natural or synthetic hormones. As an endocrine pharmacologist, you become the lead investigator pursuing the mysteries of the metabolic origins of many illnesses and disease processes that include:

- Endocrine/neural regulatory systems (eating behaviors, stress, cardiovascular regulation, diabetes)
- Aging/geriatrics (pharmacological interventions for neurodegenerative disease processes like Parkinson's or Alzheimer's)
- Cancer biology (gene therapy, hormonal regulation, antineoplastic drugs, growth factors)

Cardiovascular pharmacology focuses on studies regarding the effect certain medications have on the cardiovascular system, mainly the heart. This area of study also incorporates the endocrine and nervous systems involved in regulating function of

8

the heart and blood vessels. For example, as a pharmaceutical researcher, you could very well observe the effect of a certain drug on blood flow or blood pressure. You can analyze how certain chemicals in natural or synthetic drugs act as physiological mediators, or even on neural activity. That's a mouthful, but in other words--life-changing!

When it comes to **neuropharmacology**, a focus of pharmacology on neural conditions and body pathways, enables you to study other areas including:

- Neurological disorders (epilepsy, degenerative diseases)
- Pain disorders (analgesics, pharmacogenomics, aging, and pain)
- Psychotherapeutic drugs (antipsychotics, antidepressants, anxiolytics)
- Substance abuse (psychostimulants, sedative hypnotics, stimulants, alcohol, opioids, etc.)

If you're interested in the composition of drugs and how they interact with the chemical and molecular composition of body structures, you might focus on **molecular pharmacology**. This field emphasizes a study and understanding of biophysical and biochemical interactions between cellular organisms and drug molecules. This area of pharmacology offers those with the insatiable curiosity and desire to understand chemical and molecular biological technologies to study their effect on anatomy and physiology at a cellular level.

What about **biochemical pharmacology**? This field of pharmacology blends cellular biology, cellular physiology, and biochemistry in studying the efficacy of drug interactions with, and the influence of, chemicals on specific organisms. As a biochemical pharmacologist, you'll study and use drugs to research and uncover vital and groundbreaking information regarding biosynthetic passageways. You'll explore how certain drugs have the potential to mend and correct abnormalities within biochemical reactions and components in the human body that

9

lead to illness and disease processes. Yes, another mouthful, but can we say *exciting*?

You may decide you want to focus on **behavioral pharmacology**, studying the very potent effects that drugs can have on human behavior. Psychoactive drug research, and how certain drugs interact with learning, sleep, memory, and drug addiction, and how these drugs have consequences or benefits on human behaviors, is a fascinating field of study. You may very well be involved in devising and developing experimental interventions that focus on the function, activity, and metabolism of brain enzymes and neurotransmitters.

In fact, one of the newest disciplines in the field of pharmacy is **pharmacoinformatics**. Yes, another big word! What's with that? Anyway, this term defines the discipline that focuses on the discovery of systematic drugs and their development.

As you can see, your potential in the pharmaceutical, pharmacy, and pharmacology industries is limited only by your desire to learn, discover, and apply your knowledge in a variety of areas.

Okay, now let's focus specifically on the pharmacy industry.

Let's talk pharmacy disciplines!

A pharmacist as a generalized career choice can be broken down into three distinct disciplines:

- A pharmacy practice
- Pharmaceutics (pharmaceuticals)
- Pharmacognosy (medicinal chemistry)

Pharmaceutics is a term used to define the *discipline of pharmacy*. Also known as the science of dosage form design, pharmaceutics as a discipline relates to not only how drugs are formulated but how they're to be delivered and how their chemical components

10

react in the body. In turn, pharmaceutics can also be broken down into other sub-specialties or branches that include:

- pharmaceutical manufacturing
- pharmaceutical formulations
- dispensing
- technology
- jurisprudence
- physical pharmacy

Pharmacognosy is a term that defines the study of medicines that are culled from natural sources. The Journal of Pharmacognosy and Phytochemistry defines the field as "the study of the physical, chemical, biochemical, and biological properties of drugs, drug substances, or potential drugs or drug substances of natural origin as well as the search for new drugs from natural sources."[2]

Interestingly, this field has been recognized since the early 19th century. In the early 1800s, these studies focused on crude forms of plant, mineral, or animal materials and such used in medicine. The field is also recognized as a study of medicinal components of products found in nature, and how native cultures have long relied on their own traditional uses of these natural products, as well as focusing on safety and efficacy. For more information regarding Pharmacognosy, visit The American Society of Pharmacognosy.[3]

Pharmacy practice defines the professional role of a pharmacist in a variety of scenarios. These scenarios can include clinical interventions, patient care, drug abuse prevention, disease management, prevention of drug interactions, community pharmacy, and more.

As a pharmacist, you can focus on a number of medical practices and subspecialties that include psychiatry, surgery, geriatrics, and

---

[2] http://www.phytojournal.com/Pharmacognosy.html
[3] http://www.pharmacognosy.us/what-is-pharmacognosy/

more. That's what's so exciting about this field! Subspecialties and focal areas of study are practically unlimited based on your own specific interests.

As a pharmacist, you also have options where you can work. We'll cover this topic in more detail in **Chapter 8:** *Finding a Job*, but for now, it's important to understand that your career options can focus on the community, in hospitals or other healthcare institutions, in a managed care pharmacy, the pharmaceutical industry, and numerous federal, state/province, civil service, or military service classifications.

Did you know that as a pharmacist, you could be a staff member or even a supervisor within the:

- Department of Veterans Affairs
- Food and Drug Administration
- United States Public Health Service
- all branches of the Armed Services

At state levels, you have opportunities to become an executive officer, an inspector, or work with state health agencies where you can act as a purchaser of pharmaceutical and medical supplies for your entire state! You can even practice pharmaceutical law, or work with America's space programs in laboratories, or onboard ships, or even specialize in medicinal plant cultivation and manufacturing.

The point is that the field of pharmacy offers great diversity, not only in regard to pharmacy job opportunities but also in the field of pharmaceuticals and pharmacology as a whole. You can work in ambulatory care, long-term care, or hospital pharmacies. You could work at your local drugstore, or even as a research scientist at the Centers for Disease Control and Prevention, the United States Department of Public Health and Services, or some other federal agency.

You don't have to make a decision right now. After all, we're just getting started when it comes to exploring the world of pharmacists, pharmaceuticals, and pharmacology. So let's break this down a bit into more manageable chunks. First, let's focus on the Doctor of Pharmacy.

Doctor of Pharmacy

A Doctor of Pharmacy (Pharm. D.) is a licensed and trained individual who has undergone approximately four years of professional training and instruction. To become a pharmacist, you have to pass two exams (we'll define preparation and certification and licensure for your Pharm.D. certification in more detail in **Chapter 7: *How do I prepare for certification and licensure?***

For now, we want to focus on giving you a quick overview of what you can expect as a pharmacist.

In general, median pay (as of 2012) in the U.S. for a pharmacist is approximately $56 an hour. Not too bad, right? That amounts to approximately $116,000 a year, again not bad at all--and that's entry level. The job outlook for pharmacists (as defined by the U.S. Bureau of Labor Statistics)[4] in the next decade is anticipated to increase by approximately 14%, mainly due to the increase in the demand for prescription medications, which in turn leads to a greater demand for pharmaceutical services.

As a pharmacist, you'll have a variety of obligations and responsibilities. You don't just stand behind the glass window and count pills. Yes, you *will* dispense prescription medications, but you're also going to be relied on to provide expert advice to your customers or patients regarding safe and proper use of doctor's prescriptions. You'll also be required to answer questions

---

[4] http://www.bls.gov/ooh/healthcare/pharmacists.htm

13

regarding immunizations, overall health and wellness, and lifestyle.

Something to remember: Because many patients have more than one doctor, the pharmacist is increasingly responsible for ensuring that medications dispensed from a variety of prescriptions will not interact negatively with one another. You are a very valuable asset, not only to your patients but to the physicians and other healthcare professionals treating those patients.

So here's a basic rundown of the general duties of a pharmacist:

- ✓ Accurately and appropriately fill prescriptions, and when necessary, contacting the physician to verify instructions and/or directions in regard to dosage, frequency, and amounts of medication prescribed for patients.

- ✓ Provide proper instruction on how patients are supposed to take their medications.

- ✓ Provide guidance to patients regarding possible side effects or interactions that may occur when taking a specific medication.

- ✓ Verifying that the prescription will not interact with other drugs the patient is taking, as well as avoiding negative reactions or interactions based on medical condition.

As a pharmacist, you will also be responsible for providing patients with accurate and reliable information regarding stress management, exercise, and diet. You may be asked to provide flu shots and immunizations. You'll also be required to fill out insurance forms and interact with insurance companies in order to ensure that your patients have access to the medications and benefits of those medications that their doctors prescribe.

There's a good amount of paper-pushing as a pharmacist, and you'll need to maintain extremely accurate records, not only when it comes to insurance forms but for patient health records and similar administrative tasks. You may also need to track inventory in your pharmacy.

As a pharmacist, you will also be required to take continuing education courses (CEUs) so that you stay at the top of your profession and are up-to-date with the latest technologies and advances in the pharmacology field.

Types of pharmacists

Shakespeare once said, "*A* rose by any other name would smell as sweet," but can the same be said of pharmacists? Not exactly. As you delve deeper into the world of a pharmacist, you'll discover several different types of pharmacists. They include:

- Clinical pharmacists
- Community pharmacists
- Pharmaceutical industry pharmacists
- Consultant pharmacists

Briefly, a **clinical pharmacist** works in a facility healthcare setting such as a clinic or hospital, and contrary to popular belief, doesn't spend a lot of time actually filling prescriptions. Rather, they are part of a medical team, often accompanying physicians or other health care team members on hospital rounds, recommending medications, determining and providing oversight regarding dosage, and optimal timing of the dosage for certain medications. A clinical pharmacist can also perform medical tests and offer advice to patients in medical settings.

A **community pharmacist** is perhaps most recognizable as the pharmacist who works behind those glass windows at your local pharmacy or drugstore. In many cases, community pharmacists
15

work in chain drugstores or independently and locally owned pharmacies. The community pharmacist *does* count and dispense medications, but must also be available to answer questions that patients/customers may have regarding any prescription or over-the-counter medication. Community pharmacists are a valuable asset to society in that they're able to answer a variety of health questions and concerns as well.

A **pharmaceutical industry pharmacist** focuses on sales, marketing, or research and development, depending on preference. This type of pharmacist may also devise and oversee clinical drug trials in the development of new medications, drugs, and drug therapies, as well as help establish safety regulations and oversight of quality control.

A **consultant pharmacist** is often employed by insurance providers, as well as a variety of healthcare facilities, regarding the use of or improvement of pharmacy services when it comes to patient medications.

Pharmacy technicians

Okay, now let's take a moment to talk about job definitions. You've already been briefly introduced to the field of pharmacy and a Doctor of Pharmacy or Pharm.D. What about pharmacy technicians? What do they do, and how do their responsibilities differ from those of a pharmacist?

At its most basic definition, a pharmacy technician *helps* a pharmacist dispense medications. The job of a pharmacy technician doesn't require the educational chops that a pharmacist might need, but it is a good idea to at least complete high school and post-secondary educational programs before entering the field. We'll talk more about education basics in **Chapter 6:** *What do I have to know to become a pharmacist/pharmacy assistant/technician?*

For now, let's take a closer look at some of the most common responsibilities of a pharmacy technician. In most situations and environments, the pharmacy technician will:

- ✓ Package and label prescriptions.

- ✓ Take information from customers required to fill a prescription. This information may also come from those in the health professions.

- ✓ Be required to accurately measure medications for these prescriptions.

- ✓ Assist in organizing pharmacy inventory and letting the pharmacist know if there is any shortage of supplies and/or medications on a regularly scheduled basis.

- ✓ Assist in payment and processing of insurance claim forms as well as taking payment from customers.

- ✓ Accurately enter data regarding the customer/patient into the pharmacy computer system, including additional medications that customers may currently take.

- ✓ Answer questions by customers/patients either in person or over the phone.

As a pharmacy technician, you'll work under the supervision and licensure of the pharmacist in charge. The pharmacist is required to review all the prescriptions that you have prepared before they are given to customers.

Depending on your location, you may also be required to know how to operate automated dispensing tools and equipment when filling a prescription order. You may also be required to mix compounds or medications, as well as call physician's offices in order to authorize refills.

17

Pharmacy technicians are not limited to physical pharmacy locations for employment. You may have the opportunity to work in a number of medical facilities as well as hospitals. You may also receive additional on-the-job training in preparing medications, intravenous medications, accompanying doctors on hospital rounds, and dispensing medication to patients in such facilities.

You may wonder what other options you have when it comes to your work environment. You can count on one thing--you're going to be on your feet all day! Percentage-wise, most pharmacy technicians work in traditional drugstores or pharmacies. In the United States, approximately 53% of pharmacy techs work in such environments.[5] However, other locations do offer pharmacy technicians opportunities and options outside of the traditional drugstore pharmacy environment. For example, hospitals, supermarkets, and ambulatory health care services also provide options.

What's the difference between a pharm tech and an aide?

So what exactly is the difference between a pharmacy technician and a pharmacy aide? As mentioned above, a pharmacy technician not only engages in a variety of clerical responsibilities but can also help the pharmacist fill or refill prescriptions. It's the responsibility of the technician to help verify information, to record and update databases on the computer, as well as packaging, preparing, and labeling medication under the pharmacist's supervision.

A pharmacy assistant (also known as a clerk) typically fulfills clerical or administrative duties, and doesn't have hands-on access to refilling, filling, or dispensing prescription medication to customers/patients. For example, the main job description of a

---

[5] http://www.bls.gov/ooh/healthcare/pharmacy-technicians.htm#tab-3

18

pharmacy assistant ranges from keeping the pharmacy area clean and neat to arranging stock. You'll be expected to take care of administrative functions such as typing out medicine labels, contacting customers to notify them that their prescriptions are ready, answering phone calls, and accepting payments. A pharmacy assistant is also the go-to person for helping customers locate other medications, products, or merchandise found in the pharmacy department of the store or setting.

A pharmacy assistant doesn't need extensive training. Typically, a high school diploma is a minimum requirement in the United States. A pharmacy assistant typically receives on-the-job training from higher-ranking pharmacy employees, technicians, or the pharmacist.

So, while there is a distinct differentiation between the responsibilities (and salary!) of a pharmacy aide and a pharmacy technician, you will find that customers will very rarely be able to distinguish the difference between an aide and a technician.

A pharmacy technician and a pharmacy aide must both have skills in customer service, listening, and organization. It's also important to be detail-oriented in order to prevent mistakes when filling prescriptions. Mathematical skills are also important for anyone working in a pharmacy, especially when one of your responsibilities includes mixing or combining medications, and/or counting out pills.

Regardless, it will be your responsibility to do whatever you can to answer customer questions and ensure that they receive adequate instructions, warnings, and guidance in the taking of their medications. For this, you need to maintain an open line of communication with the pharmacist in charge. It will be your responsibility to make sure that all customer questions are answered as accurately and reliably as possible.

Shall we talk sales?

Another lucrative career in the field of pharmacy is that of a pharmaceutical salesperson. If you have a gift for gab and are highly motivated, pharmaceutical sales is an excellent avenue for those looking for even more challenges within the industry. The field of pharmaceutical sales offers exceptional potential not only in income, but in career growth and benefits. In fact, author Anne Clayton wrote a book called, *Insight into a Career in Pharmaceutical Sales.* In it, she wrote, "the pharmaceutical industry is among the largest, most stable, and fastest-growing business in the entire world." According to a global human resources and organizational consulting firm (the Hay Group), the industry of pharmaceutical sales has increased by approximately 300% in the last decade![6]

Not too bad, is it? As a pharmaceutical sales representative or agent, you'll also generate a great deal of respect within the industry. Because of your knowledge of the profession, the environment, and technologically-advanced products in your industry, your opportunities of employment in numerous work environments, your potential for career advancement, and salary earnings expands exponentially.

So who exactly can go into pharmaceutical sales? Anyone with determination and smarts can become a pharmaceutical sales representative. It's extremely competitive, active, and always challenging. Those with a background in science and/or medicine do particularly well.

So what are some of the characteristics that an employer will be looking for when it comes to pharmaceutical sales? Here are just a few:

---

[6]

http://www.science.purdue.edu/careers/what_can_i_do_with_a_major/pharmac
eutical_sales_representative.html

- Goal-oriented
- Persistent
- Ambitious
- Self-driven
- Motivated
- Great communicator (and listener)
- Personable

In addition, as a pharmaceutical sales representative, you also have to be willing to travel. Sure the money is great, but you do have to realize that you'll be spending quite a bit of time on the road, visiting doctor's offices, hospitals, and a variety of healthcare facilities and organizations.

Something to Remember: To become a successful pharmaceutical sales representative, you have to be passionate and enthusiastic about the job. If you're in it just for the money, it may not be right for you. You have to have a passion for medicine and science so that you're fully capable of understanding every single one of your products. You must be able to promote and sell those products based on your knowledge and understanding of them. (Not to mention that in order to become a candidate for the field, you'll also need to have a good driving record, be able to pass a background check, drug screening, and have a good credit report.)

If you're interested in breaking into pharmaceutical sales, it's important to begin establishing relationships with networking agents and recruiters within the pharmaceutical field. Attend job fairs, research and apply through pharmaceutical company websites, and talk to other doctors, pharmacists, and pharmaceutical district managers and sales reps currently in your area.

An additional two positions that you may find worth looking into within the pharmacy world includes **management**, and/or, if it suits your fancy, **clinical research**. The American College of Clinical Pharmacy defines a wide variety of career opportunities within the field of pharmacy, including a variety of management positions. Just a few of the leadership or management positions you can strive for include:

- Clinical manager
- Clinical pharmacy operations manager
- Pharmacy supervisor
- Pharmacy assistant director
- Pharmacy associate director
- Pharmacy director

In a management position your responsibilities and obligations increase depending on your title. However, any management position in the pharmacy field will include your ability to provide leadership, and maintain quality initiatives and standards. You'll be expected to have some involvement in clinical pharmacy consultation services and perhaps even drug informatics, depending on location. You may also be involved in the development of formulary and therapeutic drugs, or in creating, developing, and providing a wide range of information regarding drugs and medications to educational venues. This responsibility can span healthcare facilities and professionals including physicians and nursing staff. Finally, you will also be expected to mentor and teach students and medical residents in your field.[7]

Under the microscope – So you want to be a clinical research pharmacist?

Research-oriented careers in pharmacy are also an option as a career path. In fact, the global industry as a whole has seen an increased demand for clinical pharmacist scientists, especially with the changes seen in healthcare delivery around the world. As

---

[7] http://www.bls.gov/ooh/healthcare/pharmacy-technicians.htm

a clinical research pharmacist, you'll have the potential to guide and oversee a variety of clinical strategies, analyze data, and oversee design studies when it comes to pharmaceuticals, especially in the field of pharmacogenomics.

If you don't want to be hovering over a microscope all day, you don't necessarily have to when you're involved in clinical research. Many clinical research pharmacists don't work in a lab, but with real people in real-time environments. They engage in human subjects and studies and may oversee all aspects of clinical trials. Your potential involvement in research partnerships between academic fields and healthcare providers serves as a valuable bridge that transforms knowledge and research into practical applications in medicine and health care.

As you can see, the world of the pharmacist is a fast-paced field and, depending on your interests, offers increasing employment opportunities with unlimited potential. Understanding the world of a pharmacist is more than picturing a person in a white lab coat behind the glass counting out pills all day long.

While the main focus of this book is to show you how you can *become a pharmacist*, we also wanted to illustrate the wide range of choices you have within the industry. While we can't go into great detail regarding some of these professions including pharmaceutical sales representatives, pharmacy management, or clinical research due to space limitations, we do want you to be aware that the potential is out there. We urge you to continue researching these fields on your own.

In order to have the best options for success in such careers, you do want to be able to work your way up the ladder, so to speak. As a Doctor of Pharmacy, you will do just that. In many fields, experience is the key to advancement. While there are always exceptions to the rule, that basic standard will hold you in good stead. Does this mean that you have to work as a pharmacist for twenty years before you move on to something else? Not at all!

Your potential in the field of pharmacy is limited only by your own efforts, drive, and passion for the field. Exploring the field of pharmacy, pharmaceuticals, and pharmacology is just your first step on this exciting and always challenging journey.

So now that you have been provided with a brief overview of the different types of career options and job descriptions in the world of pharmacy, it's time to take this a step further. How exactly do you choose which career you want? What if you're interested in working your way up from an assistant to a technician, and then to a Doctor of Pharmacy? What if you want to skip the lower two rungs of the ladder and head right into the field as a Doctor of Pharmacy?

When it comes right down to it, you may want to know what goes on behind those doors and those windows. In the next chapter, we'll talk in more detail about the specific kinds of responsibilities that you will have based on your career choice. We'll also provide you with a number of facts and things to consider when making those choices.

Still, when it comes right down to it, do you have to choose right now? Of course not! It's all about options. That's what this book is all about--providing you with the information you need to make informed choices--whether you want to become a Doctor of Pharmacy, a pharmacy technician, a pharmacy aide, or something else in the field! You can't make a decision or a choice without knowing what to expect, the type of responsibilities you'll have, and the earning potential of every field within the pharmacist's world.

This is just the beginning. As you gain additional knowledge and information on your journey to finding out everything you need to know to maximize your career opportunities and earning potential in the world of pharmacy, you'll find that knowledge is power. That knowledge will provide you with a firm sense of direction on how you get there from here.

Chapter 2: How Do I Choose? What Can I Expect Working in a Pharmacy?

Before you make any choice regarding your career, you need to know about it, right? While there's no way to cover every potential regarding career expectations, responsibilities, work environment, or even salary, you can make an effort to learn as much about it as possible. Test the waters. Before diving right in, stick your big toe, then your foot in, and then decide.

When it comes to choosing a career path in the world of pharmacy, you can start at the bottom and work your way up, or you can go right for your Doctor of Pharmacy license. It's up to you. In this chapter, you're going to learn exactly what goes on behind that door, as well as the kind of responsibilities that you'll face depending on your career choice.

What exactly goes on behind that door?

We've all been to a pharmacy at least once, or at least that's an easy assumption to make. Whether you've gone with your parents, a sibling, a friend, or for yourself, chances are that at one time or another, you have needed medication for something. You watched the pharmacy technicians bustling around, and you probably saw the pharmacist counting out meds. You may even have wondered, when looking at shelf after shelf of pills, capsules, powders, and potential combinations, how in the world they got to the point where they knew about all those medications?

It all comes down to training and schooling. However, keep in mind that all the training and schooling in the world only takes you so far. It is practical experience and exposure to any environment that hones your skills, furthers your education and expertise, and enhances your confidence.

We already mentioned the sorts of careers that you could dive into with the pharmacy degree, from a doctor of pharmacy to a clinical research pharmacist. However, let's focus first on the responsibilities of a pharmacist.

What kind of responsibilities will I have based on my career choice?

Quick--answer this question: What is the overall goal of a pharmacist?

To count pills? Well sure, that's part of the job description, but so too is commitment. The goal of the pharmacy profession overall is to reduce or eliminate symptoms of a variety of illnesses and disease processes, slow down disease progression, and even prevent or cure a disease. In addition to those goals, the responsibility and job of the pharmacist is to dispense medications that can alter a variety of physiological processes, as determined by a physician or specialist, while at the same time minimizing health risks to your patients.

As a pharmacist, you're going to serve not only one patient at a time, which is important, but your entire community. You will be relied upon to provide reliable and accurate advice and information regarding not only medications, but on general health and wellness. As a pharmacist, you will often be called upon to refer patients to other sources of care, assistance, support, and help.

Sure, you're going to be behind that counter, that door, or that window counting pills, but you'll also spend a great deal of time monitoring and maintaining patient and customer records. The same goes for time spent educating your patients. Remember that as a consumer, every person that walks up to your window to get a prescription filled relies on you to fill it accurately. They will trust you, and it is your job to build upon that trust and provide them a solid foundation for not only their own health and well-being, but that of other family members.

Your training and education will increase your knowledge regarding physical and chemical properties and compositions of drugs on the market today, as well as those that are in production for the future. You'll learn and understand how they're manufactured and used, and be able to answer questions regarding their testing, efficacy, and purity.

As a pharmacist, your patients and customers will ask you how drugs will affect them. How does this pill or that capsule affect the body? What possible side effects can your patient expect or be watchful of?

That's what goes on behind that door. If you've ever gone to the pharmacy, chances are that you were only there for a few minutes. If you stood back and watched everything that a pharmacist does from the time he or she clocked in until they clocked out, you might be amazed, impressed, or even worried. Are you capable of doing all that? Can you keep up that fast pace and deal with the often challenging questions and issues that come up? Can you patiently listen to and answer the nearly endless patient and customer questions and calm their concerns?

That's what this book is all about. Preparing you for your career as a pharmacist. Yes, it's an exciting and demanding career, but it's not for everyone. You have to be motivated, passionate, and excited about your field. Of course, this applies to any career in which you want to be successful.

Something to Remember: The bottom line is that as a pharmacist, you must be *committed*, not only to your field, but to the public.

When you begin your journey toward becoming a pharmacist, you must carefully consider the steps involved as well as the career options you have available to you. That may take some honest self-introspection and understanding of your own abilities to not only do the brain-thinking part of it but to oversee and embrace the responsibilities of a pharmacist as well.

The American Association of Colleges of Pharmacy put together a brochure titled, "Top 10 reasons to become a Pharmacist"[8]. Let's see how many of these statements apply to you:

- I want to help people get well
- I enjoy a wide variety of career opportunities
- I like to work directly with patients
- I can benefit from the increased demand for pharmacists
- I can have job mobility, stability, and flexibility
- I want to be an important member of the healthcare team
- I want to work with state-of-the-art technology
- I am excited to be a part of major innovations in drug therapy
- I would like to be a highly respected member of my community
- I can help defend against bioterrorism

So how did you do? If you agreed with most or all of these statements, you're well on your way to having the attitude, the passion, and the positive outlook that the world of a Doctor of Pharmacy can provide you. The same applies to those interested in becoming pharmacy technicians or assistants. Some people prefer to take the road at a slower pace than others. It all depends on you.

According to the American Association of Colleges of Pharmacy, there is a great demand for pharmacists in a wide number of occupational environments. So whether you decide to go into community pharmacy, managed care, ambulatory care, or some type of government or federal agency, your options can be closely matched with your own personality, drive, and ambition.

---

[8] http://www.aacp.org/resources/student/pharmacyforyou/Pages/toptenreasons.aspx

28

Making choices - Things to remember

So now you know a little bit more about the difference between a Doctor of Pharmacy, technician, and an aide or assistant. We've briefly discussed a variety of options when it comes to choosing your career path in this field. We've briefly covered the types of responsibilities that you can expect in each of the three major occupations in the field of pharmacy, depending on your choice; that of the pharmacy aide or assistant, a technician, or a Doctor of Pharmacy.

So how do you choose? You choose by taking a number of things into consideration, which, in some cases, is based completely on your own preferences. How do you choose a career path? And what if you decide you want to change that path?

When making a choice regarding career options, be honest with yourself. Ask yourself a number of questions, and really take the time to formulate your answers. Choosing a career path is serious business. No, it doesn't mean that you can't change your mind later on, but it will help you make choices based on your personal preferences. For example:

- Choose a career path that you believe will gain you the most pleasure. We're not just talking money here, but excitement, passion, and enthusiasm. Let's face it, work is work, but when you choose work that you find enjoyable, it may not seem so much like work at all, but following your interests or passion and getting paid for it! Enjoying your work will enhance your ability to succeed at it, as well as continually advance, not only into a position in stature but in knowledge and experience.

- Does the job you want within the pharmacy, pharmaceutical, or pharmacology field limit you in any way? For example, if you don't continue or pursue your education in the field of pharmacy and you start out as a pharmacy aide, assistant, or technician, you may go no further, basically locking yourself into a "job" rather than a career. Have a goal in mind of where you want to end up. If you're happy being the pharmacy aide, assistant, or technician, then fine, but you may not feel the same way in five years. Give yourself the opportunity to advance, or to make changes that offer you additional choices within the field. Do so sooner rather than later.

- Are you willing to relocate or travel? Sometimes, job opportunities in your present location may be limited in scope or availability. Be willing to relocate to find a job that you want. Some jobs in the pharmacy field will require some travel, again depending on your geographical location. You may even be required to split your weekly hours between two facilities, or sometimes even more. Consider this and make a determination whether you're willing to do this or not.

- Choose a job that provides enough income to financially sustain you. You don't have to automatically go for the highest salary, but you do want to make enough salary to survive, pay your bills, and perhaps continue your education or gain experience in the field before you move on.

- Similar to the second bullet point, assess advancement potential, otherwise known as "Will-I-be-able-to-grow-in-this-field?" Not only do you want to gain experience in the job you choose, you want to learn, continually enhance and hone your skill set, and have the ability to pursue the positions higher up on the ladder as time passes. Your job needs to be fulfilling, not only financially, but mentally and emotionally. For this reason, look for a job position that provides the greatest diversity of experience potential, as well as potential to advance.

That being said, it's also important to be realistic regarding your expectations. Your earning potential, which will be explained in further detail in the next chapter, may differ depending on your geographical location or your preferences in regard to workplace environment. These are important factors to consider when making a decision regarding your education.

Another thing to consider as you make your way toward becoming a pharmacist is your attitude about work. If you have a positive attitude about work and have done your homework and performed due diligence researching the job descriptions and responsibilities of pharmacy assistants, technicians, or a Doctor of Pharmacy, you'll find yourself much better prepared to make those choices. Your attitude or frame of mind, as well as expectations of the jobs and your job environment also play an important role in your ability to make rational, educated, and positive decisions.

If you don't want to take the time to go to school and gain the educational chops that you'll need for the position you really want, or you aim for those based solely on financial gain, then you may need to reassess your career choices. Sure, we all want to make as much money as possible, but you also have to be willing to put forth the effort, the time, and the dedication to reach not only short-term but also long-term goals.

As discussed, the options and choices that you have regarding a career path in the world of pharmacy are only limited by your passion, your desire, and your dedication in getting there. In order to help you make the choice whether to become a Doctor of Pharmacy, a technician, or an assistant or aide, perhaps we should talk about something extremely important to all of us, regardless of career choices. Let's talk turkey.

Chapter 3: Let's Talk Turkey - How Much Can I Earn in the Pharmacy Field?

Introduction – Where's the money?

In this chapter, we want to talk about earning potential. Data for this section is focused on the job potential for pharmacists, pharmacy technicians, and pharmacy aides or assistants in the United States. However, we also try to break down potential earnings not only based on location but also years of experience.

For example, a **pharmacist** can make anywhere between $70,000 and $130,000 a year, depending on work location, experience, skills, and employer. According to PayScale.com[9], the *median* earnings for a pharmacist averages $105,792. However, on top of that, you may earn up to nearly $9,000 in bonuses as well as through profit sharing. At the end of the year, a pharmacist can earn anywhere from $81,000 to $132,000+ based on national salary data.

Note – Most of the salary info for this chapter comes from the latest data provided by PayScale.com. You may also reference the U.S. Bureau of Labor Statistics for earning potentials around the country.

Some of the most popular employers for pharmacists include locations such as CVS, Walgreens, and Rite Aid, all with a reputation of offering an approximated median salary of $122,000, although they can go as high as $140,000 a year.

You can also increase your earning potential depending on your skill set. For example, the most popular skills for pharmacists include retail pharmacy, oncology, hospital education, and long-term care. You can start out at the entry-level of these positions

---

[9] http://www.payscale.com/

earning approximately $106,000 a year, and after 20 years, earn $118,000 or more.

Let's take into consideration job location. If you live in Los Angeles, you can increase that median pay scale by approximately 4%. If you live in San Diego, increase it by approximately 10%. However, other cities, including New York City, Chicago, and Boston, may decrease your median pay scale by approximately 4% to 9%.

Remember earlier we talked about career paths for pharmacy? A typical career path for an individual entering the pharmaceutical field (as a pharmacist) is to eventually advance to retail pharmacist, a hospital staff pharmacist, or clinical staff pharmacist.

A **clinical pharmacist** can earn anywhere between $90,000 and $128,000 a year, with their median pay averaging $109,000. After bonuses and potential profit sharing, the pay scale for clinical pharmacist averages $93,000 to $134,000 a year. Some of the most popular skills required for clinical pharmacists include pharmacotherapy, pediatrics, oncology, critical care, and managed care.

The potential for increase in income at the entry level (rated between no experience and five years for a clinical pharmacist) increases by nearly $20,000 after 20 years. Those figures can be increased depending on where you live. For example, take that pay scale and increase it by 5% if you live in a location like Denver or Salt Lake City. Add 15% if you live in Los Angeles, California, or by 17% if you live in San Francisco!

While the national *average* pay for a clinical pharmacist may hover around $105,000 to $111,000 a year, you may not earn this much if you live in New York City, where that baseline pay drops by approximately 7%.[10] That's why it's so important to take into

---

[10] Estimates/data accrued on www.payscale.com

consideration your years of experience and the geographical location where you want to work to determine earning potential.

As mentioned earlier, according to the Bureau of Labor Statistics[11], a pharmacist (as of mid-2012) averaged just over $116,000 a year. The job outlook for the years between 2012 and 2022 were estimated to increase by approximately 14%, with nearly 287,000 job openings.

Now let's talk about earning potential for a **pharmacy technician**. Again according to the Bureau of Labor Statistics[12], and as of mid-2012, the median pay was approximately $27,000 to $30,000 a year or $14 per hour. Because it's considered an entry level position and doesn't require more than a high school diploma or an equivalent, you'll have lower earnings, but also great potential for on-the-job training and advancement. In fact, the job outlook for pharmacy technicians between the years 2012 and 2022 is expected to rise by approximately 20%, with over 355,000 anticipated job openings in the field.

However, keep in mind that pay scale is also determined by location, just as it is for a pharmacist. In fact, according to payscale.com, the median hourly wage of a pharmacy technician in the US is $11.67 per hour. Yearly earnings can range anywhere between $18,000 and $37,000, again depending on hourly wages and overtime pay.

A common career path for an entry-level pharmacy technician is either to advance to Administrative Assistant, Certified Pharmacy Technician (CPHT), or to continue schooling for your Pharm. D. licensure. Some of the most popular skill sets for a pharmacy technician include data entry, customer service, retail, typing, and the ability to process insurance forms. As a pharmacy technician,

---

[11] http://www.bls.gov/ooh/healthcare/pharmacists.htm
[12] http://www.bls.gov/ooh/healthcare/pharmacy-technicians.htm

you may earn approximately $20,000 to $30,000 a year at the entry-level, and after 20 years, earn approximately $36,000.

As with pharmacists, pay scale will increase or decrease depending on location. A pharmacy technician working in Los Angeles can add approximately 27% on top of the base scale ($25,000 a year) as mentioned earlier, or up to 31% if you live in San Diego. However, if you happen to live in Orlando, Florida, you may take approximately 1% to 3% off your national average earnings of $25,000 a year. Add 18% and 20% to that base scale, respectively, if you live in Boston or Portland.

As a certified pharmacy technician, and again based on educational level, you have the opportunity to earn more than a "basic" or non-certified pharmacy technician. So, as a certified pharmacy technician, you may expect a national *median* pay of approximately $12 an hour, although that pay scale can go up to over $17 an hour based on geographical location and experience.

Many certified pharmacy technicians earn up to $26 an hour with overtime, and when bonuses, commissions, and profit sharing were offered, a certified pharmacy technician can earn anywhere from $19,000 to $37,000 a year. You can start out at the entry-level making approximately $24,000 a year, and after 20 years, you'll be earning approximately $35,000 a year.

Reminder - Maximizing my earnings

We briefly mentioned several topics in the earlier section regarding increasing your income-earning potential above and beyond the base pay scale for the national average. Several of these options included over time, profit sharing, commissions, and bonuses. How typical are these possibilities in the pharmaceutical, pharmacy and pharmacology field? More plentiful than you would imagine!

Making the choice

When making a choice to become a pharmacist, a pharmacy technician, or whether to start out as a pharmacy aide to see if you like the field, take advantage of the variety of options, locations, and types of facilities you can work in. We all want to work in an environment that we prefer. When you become a pharmacist, you'll have those options.

We've provided a very brief overview of what you might expect in the different positions common to a pharmacy setting, but continue exploring on your own. The figures presented in this chapter are just the *average*--which doesn't mean you can't exceed these earnings depending on your own specific case scenario.

Yes, this section has presented a lot of numbers and figures, and we don't want to beat you over the head with them, but only present them here to give you a generalized idea of earning potential. Any job's earning potential will be based on skill level, experience, and additional education, certifications, ability to participate in bonus programs, profit sharing, as well as overtime.

Now let's move on to expectations when it comes to education.

Chapter 4: What Do I Have to Know to Become a Pharmacist/Pharmacy Technician/Assistant?

When making a decision regarding what type of education you need in the field of pharmacy or pharmaceuticals, it's not only important to know the basics but also the types of classes that will offer you the best opportunities in the field. You also need to know how to enroll in a pharmacy college. For example, how do you choose one that's right for you? What kind of credit hours are you going to need, if any? Most important to many people, how are you going to pay for pharmacy school? What kind of options will you have?
These are just a few of the questions you'll need to know about your schooling and what you can expect from it.

Education basics

We're going to break this section down into three categories, describing educational requirements to become a pharmacist (Pharm.D.), a pharmacy technician, or a pharmacy assistant or aide. We'll start with educational requirements you'll need before you can sit down and take your test for licensing as a pharmacist.

Pharm. D. educational requirements

On your journey to become a pharmacist, you'll need a doctoral or other four-year postgraduate professional degree. You can also count on having to take a variety of post-secondary coursework when it comes to education, which can include biology, anatomy, and chemistry.

Depending on your chosen pharmacy school, you may also need to pass or complete a number of requirements for admission, depending on programs. In most cases, you'll need a minimum of two years of undergraduate studies. However, do be aware that some pharmacy schools will also require you to have a bachelor's degree.

Before you even get started at a pharmacy school, you may need to complete a **Pharmacy College Admissions Test** or PCAT. We'll talk about preparing and taking tests in the next section. Also keep in mind that depending on the programs and the school, you may also be able to opt for a three-year study program. In fact, some pharmacy schools may even take a high school graduate without any undergrad or post-secondary education and put them into a six-year program!

The most prevalent subjects that you'll need to study for your pharmacy certification and/or licensure include not only chemistry but pharmacology and medical ethics. Following is a sample of the type of curriculum you can expect in order to complete educational requirements to help you prepare for pharmacy licensing.

First-year:

- Pharmaceutics I
- Biological systems I
- Healthcare delivery systems
- Pharmacy practice and experience I
- Biochemical and molecular sites of drug actions
- Pharmaceutics II
- Biological systems II
- Molecular genetics and therapy
- Public health and epidemiology
- Pharmacy practice and experience II

During your **second year**, your class curriculum may look similar to this:

- Immunology

- Self-care/non-prescription therapies
- Therapeutics I
- Therapeutics II
- Parenteral therapy externship *or*
- Pharmacy literature analysis and drug information
- Pharmaceutics III
- Management within healthcare organizations
- Therapeutics III
- Therapeutics IV
- Parenteral therapy externship *or*
- Pharmacy literature analysis and drug information

Your **third year** may look like this:

- Therapeutics V
- Therapeutics VI
- Therapeutics VII
- Nutrition
- Therapeutics VIII
- Therapeutics IX
- Therapeutics X
- Therapeutics XI
- Pharmaceutical economics and outcomes studies
- Pharmacy law and ethics

You may also be required, in year three, to focus on community pharmacy, geriatric pharmacy, sleep and pharmacological management disorders, molecular therapeutics, disease state management, pharmacy practice in women's health, pharmaceutical development, complementary and alternative therapeutics, healthcare needs of special populations, and so forth.

By the time you reach your **fourth year**, you'll be focusing on acute care clinical practices, community pharmacy, primary care, hospital pharmacy practice, as well as receiving advanced knowledge and education regarding clinical pharmacy research, the pharmaceutical industry, as well as additional electives, *plus* your doctor or pharmacy capstone.

Whew! Looks like a lot, doesn't it? Actually, the first two years of your curriculum are traditional block-program required courses. Elective courses are not offered until you get into your third and fourth years. The reason for the detailed curriculum is to ensure that you as a pharmacy student develop competencies required in this field. That's because the world of the pharmacist is continually changing. Pharmacists today are increasingly responsible for providing their public with preventive and suitable care options while at the same time meeting not only legal but ethical requirements in the practice of your field.

For those completing their basic educational requirements, but who also want to move on to more advanced positions such as research or clinical pharmacy, you may also be required to complete a residency that lasts anywhere from one to two years. A pharmacist who chooses a residency that lasts two years will also receive enhanced training and experience in a number of specialty areas that include, but is not limited to, geriatric care and internal medicine.

Educational requirements for a pharmacy technician

Many students entering school and pursuing a career in pharmacy opt to work their way up into the position of a pharmacist in order to gain experience and confidence in their capabilities. Becoming a pharmacy technician doesn't require the depth of education and training that is required of a pharmacist, but you also have a few requirements to fill before you achieve certification.

Nevertheless, depending on where you live, a number of pharmacy technicians actually learn as they go, or basically enhance their education through on-the-job training provided by the workplace. However, it is recommended, especially if you're fast- tracking your career (and to enhance your job opportunities),

40

that you complete post-secondary educational programs in pharmacy technology. You can find this type of program in most junior or community colleges, as well as vocational schools.

An educational program offered by a vocational school or community college may require that you complete approximately 600 hours of classroom instruction over a course of four to five months. Most of these programs offered by vocational schools and community colleges award certification within a year, sometimes less, although many are longer and result in obtaining an associate's degree.

Some of the specific classes that you'll need in your curriculum include record-keeping, the practice and methodologies of medication dispensing, and pharmacy ethics and law. Math studies will focus on the type of math you'll need to work in a pharmacy, as well as terminology when it comes to the names (brand and generic) of medicines, and identifying their uses and correct doses.

Not only will you be required to complete classroom education, but depending on the school, you will also need to spend a certain amount of time gaining clinical experience--otherwise known as clinical hours (more on that in just a minute).

When it comes to the curriculum, your schedule might look something like this:

- Anatomy, physiology, and terminology
- Computer basics
- Math fundamentals
- Pharmacy math (three to four advancing classes)
- Inventory maintenance
- Pharmacology (three to four advancing classes)
- Pharmacy law and ethics
- Pharmacy technician duties
- Principles of customer service

41

- Pharmacy laboratory skills
- Pharmacy computer applications
- Fundamentals of chemistry

In addition to the above classroom instruction, you may need to complete up to 200 hours of clinical experience in a real pharmacy environment. Keep in mind that class curriculums vary depending on the school, but the above will give you a basic overview of what you can expect regarding educational basics to be certified as a pharmacy technician.

What? I need credit hours--what are those and how to do I get them?

Depending on country, state, and college, credit hours applied to your curriculum courses may vary. In any health field, classroom experience is often coupled with clinical hours or practicum hours that give students real-time and environment experience in a workplace environment in their field of specialty.

The need for completion of a specific number of credit hours also applies to pharmacy technicians, although credit hours may average between 40 and 45. Obtaining real-time experience in a work environment helps to expand a student's learning process as well as give them a good idea of what to expect in the field. It's not only about observing or shadowing a supervisor or a mentor, but becoming fully immersed in your new career. This is an excellent opportunity as you learn to become a pharmacist or pharmacy technician; such experience teaches you how pharmacy personnel work together, interact with customers and patients, and what will be expected of you.

While you may groan at the prospect of having to engage in "working for free" while you complete your clinical hours, don't think of it that way. Think of it as an excellent opportunity for you to gain the greatest deal of exposure and immersion into your new career choice. No one likes to be thrown into a swimming pool when they don't know how to swim. Think of your clinical hours as a swimming aid or safety ring float that helps you grow gradually accustomed to what you can expect on a daily basis when working in a pharmacy.

You will find that of all the education you've received, those clinical hours may just be the most beneficial in providing you with the self-assurance that not only have you learned the educational aspect of your field, but in your ability to perform your job responsibilities with the utmost confidence.

Educational requirements for pharmacy aide

If you opt to start your career as a pharmacy aide, you have the option of gradually working your way up in both experience and education to higher positions. That means you can work your way up to the position of pharmacy technician or pharmacist. Because a pharmacy aide is not responsible for actually measuring or dispensing drugs, but in helping the pharmacist with mainly administrative tasks, you don't have to have a degree in pharmacy for this entry-level position.

In most cases, you can expect to be employed in a retail pharmacy or chain drugstore. Your day will involve answering phones, stocking shelves, checking inventory, making sure that medications have not passed their expiration dates, and reading medicine labels. So what exactly do you need to become a pharmacy aide?

To become a pharmacy aide you will need at least a high school degree or equivalent. In high school, it is recommended that you take subjects such as biology, chemistry, natural sciences, physics, and even life-sciences whenever possible. You also need basic computer skills.

Of course, even though you want to start out as a pharmacy aide, you can start working toward higher education that will help you step further up the rungs of the professional ladder as well as increase your salary earning potential. For this, you could work toward your associate's degree as a pharmacy technician, as well as attaining a diploma in healthcare administration.

In essence, in your job as a pharmacy aide, you're going to provide ongoing support to not only the pharmacist but any pharmacy technicians working in your location.

What kind of undergrad classes will offer me the best opportunities?

In order to become a pharmacist, and, again depending on location, you will most often be required to complete two years of undergrad course work before you can start on a four-year pharmacy program.

When it comes to education, do what you can to not only fast-track your progress, but take the types of classes that will stand you in good stead throughout your educational journey toward becoming a pharmacist. For example, the University Of Southern California School Of Pharmacy specifies a variety of eligibility requirements for application as well as required pre-pharmacy course listings that will ensure you're prepared when it's time to enroll in a pharmacy college. That means taking the kinds of classes that will be most beneficial not only for your success in enrolling in a pharmacy school, but in *performing well* in school.

For example, the University of Southern California offers information regarding their required pre-pharmacy school course list[13], which can be completed at a two-year community college or as an undergraduate student at any four-year university. This is done prior to enrolling in a Doctor of Pharmacy school program. For example, just a few of the courses on this list include:

---

[13] http://pharmacyschool.usc.edu/programs/pharmd/pharmdprogram/admission/requirements/

- Calculus
- Statistics
- General and organic chemistry with labs
- Physics with labs
- General biology with labs
- Human physiology
- Molecular or cell biology
- Microbiology
- Physiology or sociology
- Biochemistry
- Microeconomics

These suggested classes will also be offered in the number of credit hours, quarters, or semesters that will enhance your potential to being accepted for enrollment by a pharmacy school.

About pharmacy school enrollment

You may also need to take a test or two prior to enrollment in pharmacy school or college. The requirements will differ depending on the school, as well as your geographic location. For example, the American Association of Colleges of Pharmacy recommends and specifies that most students are required to take the Pharmacy College Admission Test (PCAT)[14].

This test is designed to assess not only scientific knowledge prior to beginning an education in pharmaceutics, but general academic abilities as well. This test is specifically created for enrollment in pharmacy colleges. The test is composed of nearly 250 multiple-choice questions and a requirement to complete two writing topics. In most cases, you'll have four hours to complete the test.

Let's talk a minute about this Pharmacy College Admission Test. Here's a breakdown of what you can expect in each content area:

---

[14] http://www.pcatweb.info/About-the-PCAT.php

o The **biology section** contains questions regarding concepts of basic biology as well as your knowledge of principles regarding biology. This can include generalized and broad-ranging questions about anatomy and physiology, biology, and microbiology.

o **Verbal ability** - this section determines your overall aptitude regarding sentence completion, vocabulary knowledge, and the proper way to use an analogy.

o The **chemistry section** contains questions regarding concepts and principles involving both elementary organic chemistry as well as inorganic chemistry.

o **Reading comprehension** - this section analyzes your ability to read, evaluate, and comprehend a number of science-related reading passages.

o **Quantitative ability** - this section of the test assesses your reasoning skills regarding quantitative relationships and concepts as well as mathematical processes. You can expect some basic and intermediate questions and/or applications of probability and statistics, geometry, algebra, pre-calculus, and calculus.

o **Written essay** - okay, don't groan, but be prepared! The written essay portion will ask you to write about something specific. This portion of the test analyzes your ability to use language skills in composing proper formation of sentences, language uses, and of course, English mechanics. Keep in mind that the questions in the essay section will most probably have something to do with science, culture, politics, social environments, or health. You may be asked to provide a solution to a problem, or address an opinion, providing reliable rationale or explanations as to why you feel a certain way. Make sure that you take adequate time to fully address the question or the issue presented.

In addition to the above sections, you may find a number of multiple choice questions on the PCAT test that can't quite so easily be categorized into one of the above sections. These are called *experimental multiple-choice items*, and they are generally scattered throughout the test. That's because these are under testing for potential use on *future* PCAT tests. While you won't be graded on those, and a right or wrong answer on these experimental choice questions will not affect your score, you won't know which of the questions on the PCAT are experimental in nature. Therefore, it is highly recommended and encouraged that you do your best to prepare.

We'll provide a few sample questions you may find on the PCAT.

Note - *these are not actual questions found on the PCAT test. These are only given as an example of the type of questions you may be asked!*

Keep in mind that you'll find a number of resources on the Internet where you can take practice tests in the variety of categories presented within the PCAT test exam. In addition, you can visit your local bookstore and find a wide number of test aids and books that will help you prepare not only with the basic categories, but in providing dozens, if not hundreds of sample test questions.

We encourage students to take advantage of these resources, as they will help you prepare and get in the right frame of mind before you take your PCAT exam. The PCAT is given in a multiple-choice type format.

Some questions may include topics such as:

Sample Question #1: A drug that inhibits or interferes with growth-stimulating factors like proteins are called:

    a. Antineoplastic hormones
    b. Antimetabolites
    c. Mitotic inhibitors

Sample Question #2 – What drugs are often recommended to soften and break down earwax?

    a. Antibiotics
    b. Otics
    c. Ceruminolytics
    d. Decongestants

Here's another one:

Sample Question #3 – A neuromuscular blocker is most often recommended in providing what effect?

Following are a couple of examples of the type of questions that may be asked regarding chemistry studies.

Sample question #1 – Define the name given to the horizontal rows found in a periodic table:

    a. Periods
    b. Groups
    c. Families
    d. Sets

Here's another one:

Sample question #2 – What atomic substances can't be broken down into more basic types of matter?

a. Nuclei
b. Elements
c. Molecules
d. Electrons

These are just examples, and yes, these questions are rather simple in nature, but you get the idea, right?

Topics of quantitative analysis or ability may range through a wide variety of topics/choices that include quantitative comparisons, numeric entry type questions, data interpretations, and so forth.

Quick Tip for taking your PCAT:

It's divided into a number of sections or subtests, each of which is timed. You're only allowed to work on a specific section at a time, and a time limit is given to each. Keep in mind that even if you finish one section early, you're not allowed to return to an earlier subtest or section or move forward.

One of the best ways to manage the time is to quickly peruse the questions, answer the ones that you know for sure, and then go back to the ones that may require more time in determining your answer. As mentioned, the PCAT test is divided into six major content areas that contain seven separate subtests.

When looking for sample questions for your PCAT exam, don't rely on just one resource. For example, if you type in "samples of types of questions found on the PCAT exam" into your favorite browser search bar, you're likely to get up to a dozen or more options for study guides, practice test questions, and so forth. In fact, the American Association of Colleges of Pharmacy also offers the "unofficial" PCAT practice test that includes comprehensive strategies and tools to help you prepare. You have to register, but this option provides you with a variety of practice tests in multiple-choice and essay writing, and provides a study guide that contains a huge variety of information about the contents of the PCAT and how it's structured.

In relation to the *official PCAT practice tests*, be prepared to pay some money depending on which test or tests you would like. For example, the multiple-choice practice tests range from $45 to $65, or you can purchase all three practice tests for $85. The writing practice tests range from $30 to $50, but you can get all three for $70 or all four for $90. When it comes to the study guide, you can get a downloadable study guide for $25.

Keep in mind that you'll also have to pay to take your PCAT exam. In most cases, registration for the exam ranges $75 to $210, but prices vary depending on the school and extra costs (such as late registration or utilizing paper registration forms, or additional study materials).

With that said, not all pharmacy colleges or schools require this test. In the United States, however, approximately 75% do require your scores from standardized testing such as the PCAT test. Also be aware that your score on the test when it comes to being granted or denied admission will also depend on the school or the institution.

As another example, the University of Houston (Texas) specifies its admission requirements for entrance into a Doctor of Pharmacy program[15] as follows.

First, students must have completed pre-pharmacy or prerequisite course works. Students are required to pass with a "C" or 2.0 grade point average (GPA) for all the prerequisite courses to be considered for admittance to the pharmacy program. Special emphasis is placed on math and science grade point averages. In many cases, it takes the average student between two to three

---

[15] http://www.uh.edu/pharmacy/prospective-students/pharmd/admissions-requirements/

years to complete all of the prerequisite courses for this specific university.

Second, in addition to completing the prerequisites, students are also required to take the Pharmacy College Admissions Test (PCAT), and it is recommended that a student score higher than 75% or above in the five areas of the PCAT test, defined as reading comprehension, verbal, biology, chemistry, and quantitative analysis.

Third, students may need to obtain a minimum of three letters of reference: one by a licensed pharmacist who has or is continuing practicing as a pharmacist in the United States, a letter of reference by an academic professor or advisor, and another letter of reference by a supervisor or employer, a pharmacist, or another professor.

Last but not least, you may be required to have shown an active desire to participate within your community through volunteering. The University of Houston recommends that prospective School of Pharmacy students complete at least 25 hours of voluntary or community service in order to be considered for pharmacy school admission. Why? Because the pharmacist serves as an active and well-known adviser within the community or neighborhood where he or she works. It is important to show an interest in your community, and the best way to do that is to get out and explore it, support it, and volunteer where you can to enhance the quality of life for your community.

Enrolling in a pharmacy college - how do I choose the best?

How do you choose the best pharmacy college? That all depends on you. Do you want local or are you willing to travel? Not only that, but when choosing a pharmacy school, it's important to take a handful of other factors into serious consideration. Four major factors to consider when narrowing down your choice of pharmacy school include:

- Accreditation
- Programs (especially its specialized programs)
- Faculty
- Rating

Let's break each of these down. Accreditation is extremely important. Your classes won't count unless they are accredited by professional licensing boards for pharmacists. A school can be accredited in general studies or course content, but beware the terminology. In order to utilize your coursework as meeting the prerequisites for education for entrance into pharmacy schools at major universities, or an accredited and independent pharmacy school itself, they must be *licensed by professional licensing boards for pharmacists.* That way, you can be assured that your classes count. In addition, when you go to an accredited school, you can always transfer your credits or course work to other post-secondary educational facilities.

When it comes to the faculty, make sure that your course instructors are *qualified.* They should have academic credentials for the subjects they teach as well as work experience in the field. When choosing the best pharmacy school, you'll want to make sure that your course instructors specialize in chemistry, biology, or have performed research in a related field. When a pharmacy school offers subspecialties or programs such as biochemistry, homeopathy, synthetic chemistry, and pharmacology, you'll gain not only enhanced and advanced knowledge, but broaden your network of connections within the field.

Finally, consider the reputation of the school. A number of websites rate schools based on student opinions, or by education departments. Princeton Review[16] is an example of one excellent

---

[16] http://www.princetonreview.com/college-rankings.aspx

resource to check the reviews/ratings of colleges and universities around the country. If you can, try to connect with former students or graduates through forum boards and ask their opinion regarding the quality of the education they received there. Would they recommend the school? Why or why not?

Competition for entrance to pharmacy schools can be incredibly high, and many may require you to write an essay or provide letters of recommendation. When choosing a pharmacy school, choose the best that you can. Take the time to research your options, and then narrow down your search based on your specific desires or preferences.

Never settle just because a school is closer or more convenient in regard to requirements than another. If you want to be a competitive, highly educated pharmacist, and have the confidence that exceptional training provides, take your time in choosing the best pharmacy college that will meet your needs and educational requirements.

How will I pay for pharmacy school? Do I have options?

Most students, regardless of their educational focus, also need to take into consideration the cost of schooling. However, while financing options may prove challenging, we urge students not to choose a school just because it's cheaper. Remember that in many cases, you get what you pay for. Yes, the cost of schooling in the United States and around the world has climbed to the point of being ridiculous in many cases, but there you have it.

When looking for a pharmacy school, look into and consider payment plan options. Let's explore a few of those options now. First, it's important to determine basic costs. These costs will depend on where you go to school, and whether you opt to complete your undergraduate courses at a community or two-year college, or whether you decide to take all your courses at a four-year university. When it comes to paying for pharmacy school, you also have to take into consideration whether you are an in-state or out-of-state resident. Are you planning on going to a public school or program or a private school?

Something to remember: Pharmacy school comes after your two to three years of college-level studies, and it is recommended, due to the competition in the field, that you graduate with at least a bachelor's degree. That being said, let's break down the average cost of pharmacy school in the United States.

In a public university, you can expect to pay anywhere from $3,000 to $20,000 a year for a four-year program at a university-based College of Pharmacy. Private pharmacy schools cost more, averaging between $18,000 and $40,000 a year, which can rack up to a staggering $74,000 to $160,000 over four years! However, again location is important. For example, if you opt to go to a pharmacy school in upper New York State, you may pay approximately $20,000 a year, but if you're a student going to school at the University of Southern California, you may pay an average of about $38,000 a year.

When considering a pharmacy school, carefully explore tuitions to determine an average. You may also need to add a variety of additional costs to the basic costs, which often includes books, pharmacy college admission tests, as well as varied fees charged by schools for health insurance, liability insurance, technical services, lab fees, and so forth.

Saving Money!

That being said, be a knowledgeable student. Look into options for saving money. For example, the American Association of Pharmaceutical Education provides a number of scholarships for pharmacy students. If you already work in a pharmacy as a pharmacy aide or technician, you may find that your pharmacy, depending on ownership, may provide tuition reimbursement.

Others pay for continuing education. For example, one of the most popular pharmacies in the United States (Walgreens) reimburses its employees up to $3,000 for their tuition expenses, while CVS, another extremely popular pharmacy provider in the United States, offers up to $5,000 a year for an employee who wants to go to pharmacy school, and who also promises a commitment to stay with the company for a certain amount of time.

When looking to save money on tuition, look into:

- Free college grants
- College scholarships
- Minority scholarships

For example, many schools and Colleges of Pharmacy provide undergraduate awards, scholarship for services, cash, and graduate money. Students can often access health professional loan repayment programs that will repay student loans for exchange of two years of service in areas where medical shortages are prevalent in certain states. For example, the Kentucky Higher Education Assistance Authority offers a county scholarship for pharmacy students who agree to work in one of their coal-producing counties following graduation. In such situations, the student agrees to perform one year of service in exchange for every year of tuition payment granted.

Government agencies also provide scholarship aid and/or financing. In the United States, one of the most popular is the Free Application for Student Federal Aid or FAFSA. This organization provides work-study funds, loans, and grants. Federal student loans are among the most popular way for American students to pay for their college educations. These loans are funded by the federal government and must be repaid when you finish your schooling.

Schools, depending on their location, also offer monthly automatic payment plans that can be paid by debit card, credit card, your bank account, or online options such as PayPal. Installment plans are very common in most colleges and pharmacy schools, allowing students to make monthly payments toward their education.

The bottom line is that you do have options when it comes to paying for pharmacy school. Access a variety of these options by typing in "scholarships for pharmacy school" or "grants for pharmacy school" into your favorite browser search bar and specify the name of the pharmacy school you would like to attend.

You can also call the school you're interested in and talk to their finance office staff regarding payment options. School staff are more than happy to advise students (call their financial services department) about options regarding payments, accessing and filing for scholarships, grants, loans, and so forth.

Yes, a college education and pharmacy school will cost money. However, depending on your career focus, chances are you'll be able to repay your loans or obligations in a reasonable timeframe as long as you set a schedule and stick to it.

Okay, you now have a rough idea of what you need to know to become a pharmacist, a pharmacy technician, or a pharmacy aide. You understand the educational basics required of these positions, and you have taken your undergrad classes, and have enrolled in a pharmacy school. Now it's time to turn your attention to that point in time where you're finishing up with school and beginning to prepare for your certification and/or licensure.

Hang tight--you're almost there!

Chapter 5: How Do I Prepare for Certification and Licensure?

It's important to prepare for the test you'll need to take for your certification and licensure whether you're going for your Doctor of Pharmacy or pharmacy technician position. After all, practice makes perfect. A number of tips and strategies will be offered in this chapter to help you prepare, and to give you the best chance to pass. You'll find a number of requirements that you'll need to fill before you can even sit to your certification and/or license exam as a Doctor of Pharmacy or pharmacy technician, and we'll cover those.

We also want to provide you with an idea of the types of questions you'll find on the tests that you can expect. Of course, we can't give you an example of the *exact* type of questions that will be asked, because that would be cheating! Still, we'll give you a basic idea.

Before you get started delving deeper into this chapter, we do want to suggest that even though you're in a hurry to get all the schooling over with and start your career, you do need to put aside a certain amount of time for studying in preparation for your certification or licensing exam.

Remember, we've already mentioned the Pharmacy College Admission Test or PCAT. We want to comment about the preparation you may need for the *Pharmacy Technician Certification Exam*. The Pharmacy Technician Certification Exam (PTCE) is given by the Pharmacy Technician Certification Board. The PTCE also requires you to answer test questions, approximately 90 in all. Practice exams for this test cost approximately $30, and are close in structure and organization to the actual exam. Give yourself at least 110 minutes to complete the practice exam, which is actually the amount of time that you'll be given to complete the official PTCE exam.

57

The focus of the Pharmacy Technician Certification Exam is to assess your knowledge in a variety of subjects that include pharmacology, pharmacy law and regulation, calculations, anatomy and physiology, equipment, and compounding procedures and safety. For example, we'll provide a few potential types of questions that are found the exam, broken down by category.

Pharmacology for the technician

Test questions may range from describing the side effects of vasodilators to what disease processes are not treated with certain drugs. For example:

Sample Question #1 - What type/s of medical conditions are *not* treated with Ephedrine?

    a. Congestion
    b. Incontinence
    c. COPD
    d. Hypotension

Sample Question #2 - What is the generic name for Versed?

Pharmacy Law and Regulation

Sample Question #1 - Name which government agency/agencies is/are responsible for testing drug efficacy, safety, and purity?

Sample Question #2 - What type of form is required by a pharmacist to report potential or evidenced quality issues and/or problems with a drug?

Sample Question #3 - Define at least three tenants of The American Pharmacists Association Code of Ethics.

While you may not see questions exactly like this on your test, the point is to remember that a wide variety may be asked, from the simple to the complex. Again, the majority of your questions will be multiple choice in nature.

You may also be asked to answer questions relating to equipment and tools, as well as technologies that are often found pharmacy settings. Questions may also cover medication order entry, interpretations, and filling processes and drug calculations.

The drug calculations portion of the test may be more difficult for some than others, so it is suggested that you take the practice tests in order to focus extra attention on your "trouble areas."

You may also be asked questions regarding quality insurance and inventory management, medication administration, equipment, billing and reimbursement, and ethics and professionalism.

Analytical thinking and reasoning skills may also be assessed based on the structure and type of question (and field or topic) those questions may be asked. You may believe that your answer choices are all correct in some instances. Remember that in such cases, you are expected to provide the *best* answer based on the case scenario you may be given, or your answer is designed to prioritize based on urgency in a given situation.

Most test questions aren't meant to stump you, but to assess your critical *and* analytical processing or reasoning skills.

A number of books and online resources are available to help you prepare for your certification. One popular example is available for ordering at *tests.com*[17], but you can also find adequate resources and study guides and materials at known resources such as Kaplan[18]. We're not promoting one over the other. In fact, we might even suggest that you order more than one test option for a fuller range of practice questions.

---

[17] http://www.tests.com/
[18] http://www.kaptest.com/

These practice exams often provide hundreds of questions with fully explained answers. For example, the Pharmacy Technician Certification Practice Exam Kit can be ordered from numerous sources on the Internet and offers not only 450 questions with the answers explained, but also provides exam reviews, testing tips, and a flash card system.

When purchasing books or online resources, study guides, flash cards, or practice test exams, get the latest version possible, because there is a slight difference in the scope of questions developed from year to year.

Okay, now let's move on to the type of questions that a Doctor of Pharmacy student may need to tackle when it comes to their certification or licensing.

Preparing for your Doctor of Pharmacy certification or licensing

You've got a rough idea of what you can expect in regard to testing before you enter pharmacy school, as well as brief coverage of what the pharmacy technician needs to study and practice when it comes to their certification exams. This section focuses on the Doctor of Pharmacy or Pharm. D. exam; who gives it, and how you can best prepare.

In the United States, the exam you take to become a certified/licensed Doctor of Pharmacy is called the North American Pharmacist Licensure Examination or NAPLEX, otherwise known as the Pharmacy Board Exam. The test lasts approximately 4 hours and 15 minutes, although you will typically have a scheduled 10-minute break near the end of the second hour.

Something to remember: If you require another break, your time away will be deducted from your 4 hours and 15 minutes, so make sure you go to the bathroom and take care of business before sitting down for your exam!

Note - Not to make you nervous, but if you break down 185 questions into four hours (let's say you took the 10 minute break and wiled away an additional five minutes through those four hours) your average time allowed to answer each question is 90 seconds. Now don't freak, because if you know your stuff, a minute and a half is more than enough time to read a multiple-choice question, evaluate possible answers, and choose the right one.

It is *strongly* recommended that students completing their studies and beginning their preparation for licensing spend the time (and money) to access a variety of resources to help prepare. One such online option is called Exam Master[19] (again, we are not promoting one over another, but using this site as an *example* of the types of online resources that students can access). For example, this website provides a variety of strategies, materials, and resources to help a pharmacy student prepare for licensing. In fact, this one provides over 2,000 questions followed by detailed explanations that mimic the organization and structure of the pharmacy licensing exam. It also provides flash cards as well as various score reports that allow you to focus on your trouble spots.

The NAPLEX practice exam offered by this website does its best to simulate an actual exam in style, structure, and in the variety/scope of questions asked. The topics are organized and structured based on actual percentages in the actual exam. For example, each of the practice exams:

- Simulates the NAPLEX exam format and structure
- Provides high-quality questions with explanations
- Offers different modes for tests and study practice

---

[19] http://www.exammaster.com/

- Provides detailed results and scoring reports
- Provides options to choose from three versions

Practice exams online average $25 each, or you can purchase a full range of questions and explanations that reach over 2,000 in number. Access is provided on a weekly or monthly basis, with pricing options and access ranging from one month to three months, or six months to a year. You can pay anywhere from $58 to $297 for access. You don't have to be online either, but can opt for CD-ROMs for your study purposes.

Pharmdus.com[20] is another US-based website that supports resources, study guides, and preparation for NAPLEX exams. This website provides over 1,000 review questions, study guides, and gives the student complete explanations of correct strategies and answers for reaching the correct answers. This NAPLEX preparation site also covers pharmacology, disease state management, pharmacy calculations, and more.

Students preparing for the exam can subscribe monthly, or have options for four-month access, six-month access, or yearly access. The types of practice questions include the following categories, (among others):

- Pharmacology
- Expressions of concentration
- Dose calculations
- Electrolyte solutions
- Ratios and proportions

The disease state management portions of the sample tests explore all body systems as well as conditions that include but are not limited to:

- Cardiovascular diseases

---

[20] http://pharmdus.com/

- Psychiatric anxiety disorders
- Infectious diseases
- Headache disorders
- Alzheimer's disease
- Venous thromboembolism
- Oncology

The pharmacology portions of the practice tests cover such topics that include:

- Antibacterial drugs
- Chemotherapeutic drugs
- Antiviral drugs
- Pharmacokinetics
- Pharmacological principles

The point we're trying to make here is to prepare, prepare, prepare! Rest assured that your pharmacy school will also offer a variety of resources, support, and discussions to help you prepare for your Pharm.D. certification and licensure. However, take that extra step and do what you can to enhance your chance of passing with reduced anxiety. Whenever possible, and if you can afford it, purchase a variety of books, CD-ROMs, downloads; preparation options and resources not only online, but printed materials as well. In this way, and if you spend the time, you'll find that you are much better prepared for taking your exams than otherwise.

Let's talk strategies

Remember that your schooling takes years, and by the time you're ready to graduate and start preparing for your Pharm.D. exam, the stuff you learned during your first and second year might be a little rusty. That's where reviewing comes in. Give yourself, at the minimum, a month to prepare. If you can give yourself longer, depending on your work schedule, your clinical requirements, family, or other responsibilities, do so.

Remember that there is no magic trick to passing your exam. What do you need to do to pass? Prepare! Review! Know the material! Prepare for any number of questions when it comes to studying for your NAPLEX. Some of the questions they ask can be quite surprising, and make you wonder, "What the heck?"

A number of test-taking strategies will hold you in good stead. Some sound quite simple and basic, but each of them requires focus and dedication. Here are just a few:

- Be positive. If you have taken the time to prepare, you'll feel much more positive as your testing date approaches. Yes, you'll be nervous. Who wouldn't? However, a positive attitude can help you get through some of the toughest challenges in life.

- Manage your time. When you receive each section of the test, quickly scan through the questions to get a general idea of the scope, tone, and difficulty level. Answer the questions that you know for sure first, and then go back to the others which may require more time.

- When it comes to multiple-choice questions, use the process of elimination to get to the correct answer. Discard the answers that you absolutely know are not correct. Then you can spend more time focusing on what's left to select the correct answer.

- Resist the urge to rush. Yes, you may only have a short time to answer each question, but don't think about that. Rushing can end up costing you in the end. Take the time to thoroughly read the question. Understand what it is you're being asked. Then look at the answers, and follow the suggestion listed above in regard to multiple-choice questions and eliminating the answers that you know are not correct.

- Resist the urge to cram or pull an all-nighter the day before the exam. In fact, you may consider using the day before the exam to rest and give your brain a break from all the practicing. We're not suggesting you party-hearty, but *rest*. If you've taken adequate time to prepare, you will find that taking the day off before the exam will leave you more refreshed before the test than if you spent up to the last minute quizzing yourself.

- Resist the urge to watch the clock. If you've taken enough practice tests and timed yourself (without rushing) you'll have a very good idea of your capabilities of getting through the exam sections in the time allotted.

- If you manage to get a section of the test completed before the time is up, review your answers. Make sure that all of them have been answered. Remember, only change an answer if you feel you have misinterpreted or misread the question. Your first answer is usually the right one, and too much second-guessing can only lead to confusion and doubt.

Conclusion

This section has focused on helping you to prepare for certification and/or licensure. The suggestions, tips, practice questions, and information in this section are designed to provide you with the starting point to completely and confidently prepare for those important exams. Are these suggestions the only right way to go about it? Of course not! Take it upon yourself to continue seeking resources, options, and strategies to help you not only prepare but to succeed when it comes to your exam preparation and test day.

Once you've passed your exam, you can heave a huge sigh of relief. Now you can go out and celebrate! Give yourself a pat on the back. **You have become a pharmacist, or a pharmacy technician!** Now, it's time to put your education to good use and find a job. Tips and strategies for finding the job of your dreams in the pharmacy field is the focus of the next chapter.

Chapter 6: Finding a Job

Okay, you've passed your certification and licensing exams! Yay! Now you're ready to find a job. Depending on your geographical location, finding a job as a pharmacist or a pharmacist assistant can be relatively easy, but it will still take some time, research, and consideration. In this section, we'll provide you with information on where to look for jobs based on geographic region, type of facility, and of course, job opportunities. We'll also offer you an overview of how to best prepare your resume and apply for your dream job.

This is an exciting moment in your life, and you've got the education behind you to support your goals to become a reputable and highly sought-after pharmacist or pharmacy technician. Put your knowledge and experience to date to good use. Just as you took the time to prepare for your exams, you need to take time to find your dream job. When you find opportunities, do your best to make sure that they match your overall short-term and long-term goals.

What do we mean by that? What do you want, or what *don't* you want? Are you willing to relocate? Do you want to work in a small or a large community? Are you looking for rural job opportunities or do you want to be in the thick of things in a major metropolis? These are just a few of the things you'll consider when looking for your job. So let's get started on this last part of your journey to becoming a pharmacist!

Where are all the jobs?

Pharmacists have the opportunity to work just about anywhere, whether it's in a very small town or the largest cities in the country. It depends on where you want to work, and where you would like to live. However, keep in mind, depending on where you live, that you may have to go where the jobs are. Smaller or rural communities may not have quite the demand for pharmacists and pharmacy technicians or aides as larger cities, but you may be surprised at just how plentiful jobs are even in the smallest communities.

That's because people everywhere, regardless of geographic location, will have a doctor who prescribes medications. For this reason, you'll find drugstores, supermarket chains, and pharmacies in big and small cities and in a wide variety of diverse locations. That's what makes this field so exciting. The diversity provides huge opportunities, not only in regard to your potential earnings but in adding value to a community.

Okay, so let's get started.

Remember that even though the Bureau of Labor Statistics defines job opportunities for pharmacists and pharmacy technicians and aides as a growing demand, you will also find that the field is quite competitive. In order to enhance your opportunities in the job market, we'll provide a number of tips to help make your job search a successful one.

Tip #1 In order to enhance your standing in the pharmacy world (and find that dream job you want), consider joining a professional organization. One of the most popular in the US is the American Pharmacists Association. Why? Oh, let us count the ways! Here are just a few of the most beneficial reasons to join a professional organization:

- Networking opportunities - When you join the American Pharmacists Association or similar organization, you have the opportunity to network with others in your field. You'll have access to meetings, seminars, annual events, at both chapter as well as regional meetings and gatherings.

- Enhanced career stability - When you join a professional organization in your field of study or practice, you have instant access to enhance ongoing educational options that help you stay up-to-date with the latest advancements in the field. You also receive a variety of discounts on materials, events, course works, and more (not a bad perk).

- Improving skills - When you join professional pharmacy associations, you typically have access to up-to-date technologies, information, and advances in your field through a variety of magazines and printed materials. You can also receive discounts on continuing education opportunities.

- Boost your reputation - Your membership in a professional pharmacy association can enhance your reputation and show others how serious you are about your career and your profession. As an association member, you also have opportunities to advocate for your field as well as help to develop new policies or implementations in healthcare legislation and regulations.

- Career advancement - Membership in a professional pharmacy organization also provides you with access, in addition to networking, to numerous potential job opportunities in the field. Your exposure to others enhances cross-training and specialization in a wide variety of scenarios that can help advance your career.

- Competitive edge - No doubt about it, when you join a professional association or organization in your field, you gain a competitive edge over others. Membership in such organizations or associations costs money, and many of your peers are not willing to fork over the dough. If you are, it shows your customers, peers, and competitors that you are serious about your career and your dedication to the profession.

Don't limit your membership to one professional organization; reach out not only to those found in your state or region but also to national or federal level associations. As a matter of fact, many of these associations and organizations provide listings of jobs as well as other networking opportunities. They provide access to conferences, seminars, and other events where you can literally strut your stuff! These types of perks and opportunities will place you in good stead while you seek that perfect job or continue to advance in the field of pharmacy.

We briefly mentioned that many pharmacy schools do provide services that help recent graduates land a job. They can help you write and hone your resume, provide job search assistance, and provide lists of some potential employers in the community, state-wide or nation-wide, depending on the school. They may do this actively, or also by submitting lists of graduates to local, statewide, and sometimes even national job recruiters.

For some, the transition from school environments to "real life" is a shocker, but seek guidance from school counselors or advisors to help you make this transition into your new career as a pharmacist. Rely on the experience you gained during your clinical hours training or practicum requirements to boost your confidence.

The Internet is a huge resource for anyone looking for a job. Major job search engines as well as classifieds in every city, state, and region will provide you with a wide range of job opportunities for pharmacists, pharmacy technicians, and pharmacy aides.

Something to remember: When you sign up for searches with such job search engines (think Monster, Indeed, Simply Hired, Career Builder, etc.), you're going to end up on not only the call list for the job search provider, but those that sponsor them. Be prepared to field a number of e-mails as well as phone calls from everyone and their brother for at least a week or two after you submit your application and/or apply to a job within one of the search engines. One way to get around this is to purchase a disposable phone and use that one as the contact phone when you fill in the application/contact forms for the search board. Give your desired phone number only within your actual job applications.

Tip #2 Start local. You may want to start at the local level when looking for a job. If you want to stay in the area where you're presently located, research local companies that offer pharmacy jobs. This can include your local drugstore, a supermarket with a pharmacy inside, a hospital pharmacy, as well as retail outlets. You may even consider working as a pharmacist for a physician's group, or for a federal government agency such as the VA, or even for online or mail-order pharmacies, as well as wholesalers in the pharmaceutical industry. The bottom line is that the more you know about your opportunities in your own local region, the more you'll be able to apply those opportunities to your search farther from home.

Tip #3 - Another option for finding your dream job as a pharmacist or as a pharmacy technician is to hire yourself a **recruiter**. Depending on your already busy schedule and obligations, you may not have time to spend the hours, days, or even longer looking for work, following up leads, and so forth. Recruiters do that for a living. In fact, an experienced recruiter can save you not only time, but money in your job search, because he or she will carefully match your specifications, goals, and preferences when seeking a position for you.

Tip #4 - Maintain communication. So let's say you've sent an e-mail or your resume to a specific employer. Your job search isn't over. You can't just sit around and wait, and wait, and wait. Be proactive! Before you send that email off, make sure you're sending it to the right department or person within the company or business. Take the time to research the person who does the hiring or the name of the human resources department manager responsible for hiring new employees. Get their name, and then look on the website to see if you can find their department email address there. If you can't, go ahead and send the e-mail to the general business, with "attention to" to John or Jane Doe or

71

whoever is in charge of recruiting for the human resources or hiring department.

After several days, send a follow-up note, reminding them that you sent your resume on so-and-so date and then again thank them for the opportunity to apply for the job. You can even go in person if you live locally.

Note – Don't be a pest! It's one thing to send a follow-up email or visit. That is expected. However, don't make a pest of yourself. One or two follow-ups is generally adequate to test the waters, so to speak. If you don't hear anything within a couple of weeks, move on.

Following up on your resumes, queries, and e-mails in your job hunt search can prove especially beneficial and shows potential employers that you are proactive in seeking the job you want.

Let's talk resources

Depending on your geographic location, you may have access to a wide variety of resources when it comes to finding a job in the facility environment *and* geographic region in which you're interested. In the United States, we can name half a dozen off the top of our head, but be diligent and do your own research to increase the number of resources on your job-hunting list. For example:

Pharmacist Jobs (www.pharmacistjobs.com/) is one resource that lists pharmacist and pharmacy technician jobs throughout the United States. From this website, you're able to compare salaries based on geographic region, as well as search your dream job by typing in the type of facility or facility environment in which you'd prefer to work (drugstore, supermarket, retail location, hospital pharmacy). You'll also have options to upload your resume. (We'll talk more about preparing your resume in just a bit.)

RX Career Center (www.rxcareercenter.com/) is another excellent resource for job searching not only pharmacy jobs, but position openings for pharmacy technicians, as well as other professional fields in the pharmaceutical industry. This job hunting board also provides numerous settings for environment and includes clinical, retail, and hospital settings. Base your searches on keyword insertions for category and location.

Pharmacy Postings (www.pharmacypostings.com/) is a well-known search engine for those searching for pharmacist jobs as well as other traditional positions within the pharmacy/pharmaceutical industry. This job board allows you to search by position, category, and state.

RX Insider (www.rxinsider.com/) enables users to create an electronic portfolio, and provides a variety of software, networking, and marketing options and software to enhance your search in the pharmacy field.

RPh On the Go (www.rphonthego.com/) happens to be one of the most popular staffing services companies in the pharmacy industry. This website allows you to not only search pharmacy jobs based on setting/environment, but also in government and military installations.

Pharmacy Staffing (www.pharmacy-staffing.com/) is yet another professional pharmacy staffing agency. It provides access to temporary and permanent pharmacy jobs, as well as placement programs for pharmacists and technicians in numerous environments: retail, hospital, long-term care, clinics, governmental, as well as specialty pharmacies.

These are just a few of the most popular job search opportunities in the United States, but there are more. Look for such organizations and opportunities in your region. You can begin your search by accessing local jobs search engines on the Internet and go from there.

Next, we'd like to talk a moment about the pros and cons in working in various geographical settings. In **Chapter 3:** *(Let's Talk Turkey - How Much Can I Earn in a Pharmacy Field?)* we discussed potential earning scales throughout the country, depending on geographical region. This applies anywhere and may be something that you want to take into consideration when looking for your new position as a pharmacist. While a few thousand dollars a year difference in salary may not matter to some, it does matter to others. Take a look at the following list of average pharmacy salaries based on geographical location. The following are just a few of the examples provided at *RXSalary.com*[21]

Location	Low salary	Average salary	High salary
California	$118,160 - Visalia	**$132,710**	$147,840 – San Jose
New York	$106,400 - Utica	**$116,272**	$138,880 – NY city
Wyoming	$107,744 - Cheyenne	**$108,528**	$109,528 - Gillette
Nevada	$107,856 - Las Vegas	**$115,640**	$123,536 - Sparks
Arkansas	$98,896 - Little Rock	**$100,867**	$103,040 - Fayetteville

These are just a few examples of low, average, and high salaries based on geographic locations in the US. The website listed above (RX Salary Calculator) also offers an option where you can estimate potential salary earnings by typing in years of

---

[21] http://www.rxsalary.com/Pharmacist-Salary-by-Geographical-Location.asp

experience, your degree, the position you're looking for, practice setting (environment), specialty, and geographical location.

While money is great, also take into consideration the environment where you work. You may not make as much working in a local drugstore that you might in a hospital, but maybe you prefer the pace or the people or the atmosphere. The same applies to your geographic location. You may prefer more rural areas to cities, or vice versa.

When determining potential earnings as an important aspect of your job search, don't forget that your earnings may be enhanced by extras or perks based on employer and scenario. Bonuses, stock options, and other opportunities as previously mentioned will bump up your earnings as well.

To take advantage of the best earning potential as well as facility and geographical location that you want, you need to literally put your best foot forward. What do we mean by that? We mean taking the time to prepare your resume and promote yourself without going overboard or, at the opposite end of the spectrum, not presenting yourself in a manner that will enhance your job and career expectations.

Preparing your resume and applying for your dream job

Most of us hate the thought of creating a resume. Opinions regarding resume development vary from "they're stupid" to "they're intimidating." Who reads resumes these days? You can bet that hiring managers and human resources departments do. In this section, we'll focus on the basics regarding resume creation and provide you with a few tips and strategies to create a professional resume.

Why is a resume so important? At its most basic purpose, a resume is your first introduction to a potential employer. Remember that first impressions *do* count. Don't underestimate the power and the potential that a well-prepared resume can offer in your job search to become a pharmacist, a pharmacy technician, or even a pharmacy aide.

Your resume is your first chance to make that good impression, as well as capture the attention of a potential employer. However, it's also important to know *why* you need to prepare your resume to do so. Here's an eye-opener--you may have only *a few seconds* to capture the attention of a potential employer, a hiring manager, or that person in the HR department responsible for hiring employees. Why? Because in most cases, these individuals are overwhelmed with a constant influx of paper and electronic resumes.

Think of it this way. How long do you watch a specific television show before you decide to change the channel? How many pages into a book do you get before you decide whether you want to continue reading or not? Probably only a couple of minutes, or at most a page or two. Think of your resume the same way. You have to get them from the get-go.

A professional resume will provide the information that an employer is looking for. It will also enable you to stand head and shoulders above your competitors. You've worked hard to attain your degree and certification, so spend just as much dedication and effort in creating your resume.

That being said, you'll find two major methods for drafting your resume most effective. Resumes are classified as:

- Functional
- Chronological

A *chronological resume* is more suited to a job hunter who already has a relatively stable work history. This type of resume is also best suited to someone who has been in the field, especially for those who have risen in the ranks or achieved higher position levels. For example, in this situation, it might apply to a person

76

who started out as a pharmacy aide who worked his or her way up to pharmacy technician, and who is now looking for a job as a pharmacist.

A *functional resume* is often recommended as a format for recent graduates, or for someone desiring to make a career change. This type of resume gives you the option to focus on or highlight specific abilities, knowledge, and skills. This is also the type of resume that you may prefer if you're entering the pharmacy world for the first time, despite a past work history (and perhaps from a different field or industry).

Regardless of which type of resume you choose, you'll find commonalities to both. It is highly recommended that you include the following information into either type of resume.

It may seem obvious, but you'd be amazed at how many people *forget to insert their contact information* on their resumes! That means your telephone or cell phone number, your e-mail address, *and* your physical mailing address. Don't forget to double-check to make sure this information is accurate.

You also want to include a *summary* (keep it brief!) of your expertise or skills. This doesn't mean bragging, or "enhancing" your abilities (read lying), but stating your areas of expertise or experience, and some of the skills that you have learned along the way that will apply to the job position you're seeking.

Don't forget to include your *work history*, and in doing so name your former job titles, company, and responsibilities. Insert accurate dates where you've been previously employed.

Both types of resumes should include your *education history* as well as *qualifications*. That means not only your basic education, but any certifications and/or licenses that you have acquired since graduation. Don't forget to mention skills you have that are *relevant* to the position you're seeking. These may include such things as knowledge regarding hardware systems, software, or other technical skills that may focus on computer functions.

Last, but not least, we should emphasize *honesty* when creating your resume. Don't be tempted to fudge the dates you worked, the skills you acquired, or the position you had. Remember that fraud is illegal, and if your potential employer finds out that you misled or otherwise lied on your resume, you can pretty well kiss that job goodbye, as well as ruin your reputation. While you might not think they'll check, always assume that they will. Chances are, especially when hiring in the pharmacy fields, you can pretty much guarantee that they're going to do a background check and make sure that all the I's are dotted and the T's are crossed.

You'll find a vast number of resources for creating resumes on the Internet, not only from major job search engines but also from professional organizations. You can also access a huge variety of resume samples that will help you format and determine exactly what type of information, and how much of it, you should insert into the resume.

Remember that your resume is your first opportunity to present yourself to a potential employer. Give it your best shot. Resist the urge to just throw together a resume and hope it flies. Rather, take the time to carefully compare your resume draft with other professional samples available for comparison on the Internet. Let the resume sit for a few days after you've drafted it and then go back and read it again. Does it make sense? Does it flow? Does it provide the information required by the company you are applying to? Does it have any formatting, spelling, or grammatical errors?

At this point, we strongly urge anyone developing a professional resume to have the resume edited by a professional copy editor prior to sending it out. If you don't want to go that route, at least provide a copy of your resume to friends, peers, or even your old school professor, or someone else you trust to give you *honest* and constructive feedback.

Remember that employers often spend less than ten seconds perusing a resume. In fact, according to one major job search engine, an employer rarely spends even a minute reviewing a resume. Typically, they take approximately *6 seconds* to make a determination whether they will put your resume in the "maybe" pile or the "probably not" pile for the position up for grabs. Why so little? After all, you may have spent days, or even weeks, creating and polishing your resume! It seems rather rude that someone wouldn't give you at least the same consideration at the other end of your efforts.

However, keep in mind that human resources staff, hiring managers, and employers are inundated with dozens, if not hundreds, of resumes on a weekly or monthly basis. They may be overwhelmed with the number of applicants applying for a single job position. The first round of reviewing resumes is going to weed out the potential from the non-potential candidates.

So what exactly are they looking for?

- Structure.
- Delineated sections (use of bold headings and indentations, bullet points, and short sentences).
- Recruiters typically focus on current and/or previous job title, positions, and employment dates. If the jobs you've held don't match the position that you're applying for, you may need to gain some experience in the field. Not always, but sometimes.
- Impact. You want your resume to be not only effective but utilize potential for impact. How do you do that? Use action words (if you're not sure what defines an "action word" look it up).
- Grammar and spelling. If you don't take the time to spell words correctly or create proper sentence structure, you can inadvertently give the impression that you're sloppy or that you just don't care. Yes, typos can slip by sometimes,

but that's why it's important to proofread, proofread, proofread! Don't rely on spell checkers in your document programs.

Remember that this brief overview regarding resumes is just that, an overview. Your resume will separate you from a *maybe* to a *potential* to an *excellent fit* for the company or employer. Your resume sets you apart as qualified for the position under consideration. If your resume passes the first scan or round of reviews, chances are the hiring manager, employer, or HR person will put it in a separate stack and look at it more thoroughly after the initial review. Remember that a recruiter isn't necessarily looking just for *talent* on your resume but *capability,* as well as qualifications and potential.

Conclusion

You're well on your way to obtaining your dream job of becoming a pharmacist. Throughout this book, we have striven to provide reliable, accurate, and applicable strategies, tips, and information to help you become a pharmacist, a pharmacy technician, or a pharmacy aide. You have begun your journey of exploring the field of pharmacy, which should help you differentiate between the overall job descriptions and responsibilities of individuals who work "behind the glass."

You have gained an understanding of exactly what goes on behind the door of a pharmacy office, and the kinds of responsibilities that apply to a pharmacist, a pharmacy technician, and a pharmacy aide. We've also mentioned a number of aspects of the career that you'll need to consider when making a choice of what position or field in the pharmacy world you want to work.

You have a rough idea of the kind of money you can make in the field, whether you work as a Pharm.D. certified pharmacist, a pharmacy technician, or even if you decide to venture into pharmaceutical sales, management, or clinical research. As you've seen, the opportunities and options in this field are many and offer continual career advancement depending on your ultimate goals.

We've provided a brief overview of the educational requirements and basics that you'll need not only before you enter Pharmacy College but how to get there. Take the time to explore every aspect of your education and access as many resources as possible when preparing for certification and licensure.

This is just the beginning of your journey to becoming a pharmacist, a pharmacy technician, or a pharmacy aide or assistant. We've covered all the basics when it comes to what you should know--from job descriptions to clinical training hours, degree requirements, and what you need to know and how to prepare for your Pharm.D. exams and licensing. We've provided information regarding schools, potential salary earnings, and how to put your best foot forward to make a wonderful first impression when you send out your resume.

Finally, do whatever you can to maximize not only your earning potential now but into the future as well. Enhance your career opportunities by taking your studies seriously and doing whatever you can to continually advance your knowledge not only of what goes on behind the glass but in the entire field of pharmacy, pharmaceuticals, and pharmacology. In today's economy, job competition is fierce, and the more you do to ensure your success as you begin your journey to become a pharmacist, the better off you'll be in the long run.

Most importantly, we hope that this book has encouraged you to realize the great challenges, potential, opportunities, and excitement that a career in pharmacy can offer you. If you're up for the responsibility and desire to help people every day, and want to provide a very valuable service within your community, you can become a highly respected and sought-after pharmacist no matter where you live.

We wish you well as you begin your journey to become a pharmacist, a pharmacy technician, or a pharmacy aide. We encourage you to never to be satisfied with the status quo. As you gain knowledge, experience, and greater and deeper understanding of this field, you will likely exceed your original goals and expectations and benefit from one of the most lucrative, meaningful, and satisfying professions out there.

Good luck!